From East to West

From East to West

THE WESTWARD MIGRATION OF JEWS FROM EASTERN EUROPE
DURING THE SEVENTEENTH AND EIGHTEENTH CENTURIES

by *Moses A. Shulvass*
SPERTUS COLLEGE OF JUDAICA

Wayne State University Press   Detroit   1971

1626238

to Phyllis and Ruth

Other books by Moses A. Shulvass

Die Juden in Würzburg während des Mittelalters 1934
Rome and Jerusalem (Hebrew) 1944
Chapters from the Life of Samuel David Luzzatto (Hebrew) 1951
Jewish Life in Renaissance Italy (Hebrew) 1955
In the Grip of Centuries (Hebrew) 1960
Between the Rhine and the Bosporus 1964

Contents

Preface

MIGRATION has been a major factor in the life of the Jewish people throughout the two and a half millennia of their dispersion. And yet, the history of the Jewish migratory movements has not been fully explored in Jewish historiography. While the Jewish migratory movements in the nineteenth and twentieth centuries, and especially immigration to the New World, have attracted the attention of scholars, earlier such movements did not. In the present book I propose to discuss such a movement of an earlier period, that from Eastern Europe to the countries of the West, from its inception at the beginning of the seventeenth century to the dissolution of the old Polish commonwealth. Since this book deals with the history of a Jewish migratory movement, it should be understood that unless otherwise indicated, the terms emigrants, immigrants, and migrants refer to Jews.

I want to acknowledge the wholehearted collaboration of my wife Celia, who shared with me all the trials which confronted me in the preparation of the manuscript. Her devotion and support accompanied all my work. I wish also to express my gratitude to my friends Leonard C. Mishkin and Ludwig Rosenberger for placing many rare books and pamphlets in their collections at my disposal when I did the research for this book.

Moses A. Shulvass

Department of Graduate Studies
Spertus College of Judaica
Chicago, September 1970

Introduction

I

JEWISH historiography has not yet succeeded in clarifying satisfactorily how and why the largest Jewish population known in history came into being in Eastern Europe. It is, however, commonly accepted that the main factor in its emergence was the immigration to Poland and Lithuania of Jews from the West, primarily from Germany. In addition, a process of inner migration developed in the old Polish commonwealth that resulted in the transfer of masses of Jews from its western to its eastern and southeastern regions.[1]

All these movements continued until about the middle of the seventeenth century. In fact, the Thirty Years' War brought a new wave of Jewish immigrants from Germany to Poland and Lithuania.[2] This *Drang nach Osten* came to a standstill during the years 1648-1660, when Polish-Lithuanian Jewry suffered the great calamities of the Cossack massacres and the Muscovite-Swedish invasion.[3] At this juncture began a process of major importance in the history of the Jewish people, a "drive west" of Jews from Eastern Europe. True, the new Jewish settlements in Western Europe, which began to develop at the close of the sixteenth century, were established by immigrant Marranos from Spain and Portugal (Sephardim). The Jewish settlements in the Western Hemisphere were also founded by Sephardic Jews. But all these communities became mass settlements only as a result of the successive immigration of Ashkenazic Jews, primarily from Eastern Europe.

The stream of Eastern European Jews to the western countries put an indelible mark on the life and culture of the then small native Jewish communities of Western Europe. The immigrants from Eastern Europe became a major problem in Western Europe during the eighteenth century when large numbers of poverty stricken Jews poured in from Eastern Europe, despite many obstacles. In fact, they had become an issue already several decades before the fateful year of 1648, to the extent of being reckoned with in the literature of the time.[4]

Though the integration of the new immigrants in western Jewish society was not easily achieved, their impact on Jewish life in the new countries became more and more visible. They greatly influenced religious life. A certain way of building ritual baths that became customary in Hamburg was introduced by rabbis who had escaped from Vilna in 1656.[5] Wooden synagogues built in southern Germany by immigrant Jewish craftsmen from Poland vividly resembled similar structures in Poland.[6] Immigrants from Poland also helped to strengthen commerce between their former homeland and Germany and Holland.[7] In general, the impact of Eastern European Jewry on Jewish life in Western Europe has yet to be described.

The Eastern European migratory movements during the period 1600-1800 have so far received only scant attention from Jewish historians. A book dedicated to the history of Jewish migratory movements of all times does not even mention the westward migrations of Jews from Eastern Europe before 1800.[8] Even those scholars who grasped the significance of the year 1648 in the history of Jewish migrations mentioned it but casually and very briefly.[9]

II

In the following chapters I propose to describe the course of the Eastern European Jewish migrations during the seventeenth and eighteenth centuries to countries west of the Polish commonwealth: the Hapsburg monarchy (Austria, Bohemia, and Moravia), the Germanies, France, England, Scandinavia, and the Americas.[10] An important characteristic of the whole movement is that not all the emigrants settled in Silesia, Moravia, or eastern Germany, the countries bordering on Poland. Some wandered through other countries of Western Europe before settling permanently. To be sure, many emigrants left for northern Germany and Holland by boat from the harbors of Lithuania and Kurland, and it is even possible that already in 1648 or 1649 a boat with Ukrainian refugees reached England.[11] But most of the emigrants who arrived in France, Holland, and England, first entered Germany, and from there proceeded farther west. Those Eastern European Jewish emigrants who reached North America during the eighteenth century did not go there directly from Poland. They usually lived for some time in Holland or the British Isles.[12]

This fact turned all of Western Europe into one vast area where Jewish emigrants from Eastern Europe felt "at home." We find emigrant rabbis accepting successive positions in various parts of the new immigration area.[13] The artist Solomon Bennett, who lived in Polotsk, went from there to Riga, from Riga to Copenhagen, and then to Berlin, before settling permanently in London.[14]

All of Western Europe was also a vast new homeland for large numbers of poverty stricken Jews from Poland and Lithuania who wandered over the Continent during most of the seventeenth and all of the eighteenth century. They were called in the official language of the various governments in the Germanies *Betteljuden* or *Schnorrjuden* (beggar Jews). Among them were wanderers from Germany and Bohemia as well. But there is no doubt that most of the time Polish and Lithuanian Jews constituted the majority.[15] The *Betteljuden* remained perpetual wanderers because of the stubborn, though mostly unsuccessful, efforts of the various governments to turn them back.[16]

The sources offer descriptions of both individuals and

groups of families with lifelong records of wandering, who penetrated the West as far as southern France.[17] The sources also show beyond doubt that the number of *Betteljuden* was large. The refusal of the governments to admit them to the cities sometimes drove them to acts of violence. Some even joined the robber gangs then plaguing the Germanies. The *Betteljuden* ultimately became an international problem, and efforts were made to place the matter on the agenda of the all-German diet that met at Regensburg in 1736. Suggestions for dealing with the problem included their expulsion from the Germanies. Simultaneously, permission was to be given to wealthy Jews to send aid to their brethren in other countries in order to limit the need for emigration.[18] These measures, however, turned out to be inadequate. The wandering Jews from Eastern Europe remained a bizarre part of the Jewish population of the West until emancipation made it possible for them to become citizens of their various cities and states.[19]

III

The uprising of the Cossacks in 1648 and the Muscovite-Swedish invasions that followed were the forces that started the large scale westward migratory movement among the Jews of Eastern Europe. But they were not the main cause of this great uninterrupted movement. The Ukraine was re-settled by Jews in the decades following the riots.[20] It also seems that a very large group of Jews, who had fled from Poland to Silesia in 1655 to escape the horrors of the Swedish invasion, returned to Poland as soon as the war was over.[21] As yet unproved, and probably incorrect,[22] is the opinion voiced in historical monographs that the later riots of the Cossacks in 1768 and the massacre of the Jews of Uman drove new masses of Jewish emigrants to Western Europe.[23] The theory that pogroms are the main factor which creates waves of Jewish emigration is exaggerated.[24]

14

The reason why large numbers of Jews streamed westward throughout the seventeenth and eighteenth centuries was twofold: (1) the progressive decline and pauperization of the Polish commonwealth, and the perpetual persecutions of the Jews that resulted from them, and (2) the fact that during this period Western Europe began to develop into the political, economic, and cultural center of the world. Therefore, Jews who succeeded in overcoming the formidable obstacles of settling in Western Europe, were able to live under politically more secure and economically much more favorable conditions.

The attitude of the western states and their Christian populations toward the immigration of Jews from Eastern Europe varied from time to time and from place to place. It has been widely believed that the devastation caused by the Thirty Years' War, the political interests of the absolutist rulers, and a rising commercial capitalism created in Western Europe a climate favorable to Jewish immigration.[25] All these factors, however, are not a sufficient explanation of the phenomenon of Jewish migratory movements in their totality. While immigrants arrived in Berlin and Frankfort on the Oder in Prussia uninterruptedly,[26] we do not find them in the city of Brandenburg.[27] The same situation prevailed all over the Germanies. In certain cities we find considerable numbers of immigrants from Eastern Europe, while in other towns of the same area we miss them. Local conditions evidently were an important factor in formulating a policy toward Jewish immigration.

Lately an attempt has been made to explain the varying attitudes of the governments of the Germanies toward Jewish immigration in the following manner: during the decades immediately after the Thirty Years' War they looked favorably upon Jewish immigrants, who helped to repopulate their devastated countries; in the eighteenth century, however, when the population had increased again, they began to discourage Jewish newcomers from the East.[28] This theory also turns out to be too general when it is analyzed in the light of the facts. According to this theory, for instance, it would be impossible to explain why Saxony admitted few Jews up to the end of the first third of the eighteenth century. And precisely at the time when, in accordance with this theory, Jewish immigration should have been stopped, Saxony began to admit more Jews and its Jewish population began to grow.[29]

Another factor that seems to have been essential in formulating the attitude of the states was the number of immigrants. As long as small groups of refugees came, they were received with tolerance, and their arrival was not seen as a specific danger. But the deeper we progress into the eighteenth century, the more unbearable was the general situation in Poland and the more numerous were the emigrants. This mass immigration became a concern to the western governments.[30] We find a striking illustration of this fear in Silesia. When in 1737 it looked as if the Jews were going to be expelled from Lublin,[31] the Silesian authorities took hasty precautions to stop refugees from entering the country.[32]

The efforts of the western governments to halt Jewish mass immigration, or even to control it, turned out to be futile. They then began to issue laws limiting the size of the native Jewish population. The purpose of these laws was to prevent Jewish communities from extending a helping hand to *Betteljuden* in their effort to settle in a new country.[33] Throughout the eighteenth century numerous censuses of Jewish populations were taken in many towns and states to spot "illegal" Jews.[34]

All this accounts for the impossibility of formulating an all-embracing principle to explain the phenomena connected with the arrival of Eastern European Jews in Western Europe during the seventeenth and eighteenth centuries. Changing conditions made Western Europe a chessboard of areas settled by Jews and areas that remained *Judenrein*. But in its totality, the Eastern European immigration of that epoch completed on a large scale the recolonization of Western Europe by Jews, which had been initiated on a much smaller scale by the earlier arrival of the Sephardim.

16

Of paramount importance in the history of a migratory movement is the degree to which new arrivals become integrated in their new countries, and how many do not take root in the new environment but return to their former homes. The sources show that most of the immigrants who did return—and they were few in number—were members of rabbinic families who had obtained rabbinic positions in Eastern Europe.[35] It seems that not enough rabbinic posts were available in Western Europe for the many sons and sons-in-law of the numerous rabbis who left the Polish commonwealth for the West. But far more frequently we encounter complete integration with all its phenomena: cultural adjustment, economic success, and intermarriage with members of the native Jewish communities.

CHAPTER ONE

Before 1648

I

LITTLE information is available about Jews who emigrated as individuals or in groups from Poland to the West before the end of the sixteenth century. Philip Ferdinand, an apostate from Poland who served during the second half of the sixteenth century as a professor of Hebrew at universities in England and Holland, was certainly an exception. The same holds true of a Jew from Posen who lived in Budvitz (Moravia) in 1562.[1] Somewhat more often, rabbis from Poland accepted positions in other countries. The famous preacher Ephraim Lunchitz and the great mystic Isaiah Horovitz are good examples; both became rabbis in Prague early in the seventeenth century.[2]

However, as the seventeenth century progressed, more and more Jews began to leave Poland to emigrate to western countries. A decade before the year 1648, the sources tell us of Polish Jews who took frequent trips to Bohemia and the Germanies.[3] The sources also relate, for the first time, the reasons why Polish Jews began to migrate to other countries. It was obviously the economic motive that drove them from their homes, even before the fateful year 1648. One man left Poland for Turkey "because of economic stress"; another fled to Amsterdam "because of his financial situation."[4] The second man, incidentally, returned but was compelled to emigrate again "because of the war turmoil in the Polish lands." The peregrinations of this two-time emigrant from the vicinity of Lemberg exemplify the conditions that drove Polish Jews from their homes even before 1648, and which became more compelling in the wake of the great uprising of the Cossacks and the Swedish invasion.

Economic stress was also the cause of the emigration of Talmudic scholars, who began to leave Poland for the West, where they could find employment as teachers. Poland was full of Talmudic scholars who did not occupy rabbinic positions but were active in various areas of business. Already in the early decades of the century a trustworthy source tells of many rabbis who lost their fortunes and went to the Germanies to become teachers.[5] Thus a part of the professional intelligentsia was also compelled to leave for the West in search of a livelihood.

An additional factor that encouraged emigration to the West was a softening of the attitude of some governments toward Jewish immigration. In the free city of Danzig, for instance, where they were not officially permitted to dwell, we nevertheless find hundreds of Jews staying permanently, even before the close of the sixteenth century.[6] Similar situations existed in Altona and Frankfort on the Oder. In Altona a Jewish community was established around 1600; among its first members were Jews from Poland. In Frankfort on the Oder a Jewish settlement was reestablished about 1635 by the admission of a number of immigrants from Poland.[7]

II

Economic stress was not the only cause of the westward migration of Jews from Poland; the economic opportunities of the wartime years 1618-1648 also induced them to emigrate. Wealthy merchants settled in Vienna, where one even became a court-Jew.[8] The several hundred Polish Jews tolerated in Danzig were active in international trade. A not negligible number of Jews went to Bohemia, Moravia, and Germany to act as suppliers to the many armies perpetually marching across the land.[9] Even an immigrant who worked in western Germany as a teacher, and for a certain time as a rabbi, became a *marketender* (sutler).[10] In our sample list gathered from various sources of 20 emigrants of the 1630s and 1640s, we find 11 rabbis and teachers, 2 printers, and 7 merchants. At least six emigrants who settled in Vienna became houseowners.[11]

It is likely that already at this time numbers of poor, homeless Jews (*Betteljuden*) from Poland were wandering over Germany. Among the hundreds of *Betteljuden* wandering in Alsace during 1620-1651, we can identify 14 men and one woman as having come from Poland.[12] Johannes Buxtorf the Elder reports it was well known that German Jews extended a helping hand to their poor wandering brethren but were reluctant to accept them in their midst. He also quotes the following epigrammic rhyme about a wanderer then current among German Jews:

> The first day he is a guest,
> The second day he is a pest,
> The third day is his last.

> *Bejom rischon orach,*
> *Bejom scheni torach,*
> *Bejom schelischi borach*
> (or *sorach*).[13]

This epigram reflects a time when *Betteljuden* had not yet become a drastic problem to be dealt with by the governments, but had begun to be a nuisance to local Jewish populations. We will see that in later decades large numbers of Polish Jews were found among the wanderers.

III

The immigrants arrived from all parts of the Polish commonwealth. They came from Posen and its vicinity, from the region around Lublin, from Volhynia, and from the south-east, around Lemberg. They originated from both small towns and big cities. But it seems that a larger proportion came from cities, such as Cracow and Posen, and to a lesser degree Lublin, than from small towns.[14] This can be explained in part by the fact that a considerable number of emigrants of the period before 1648 were rich merchants, who naturally lived in big cities. It is possible, however, that this phenomenon was a result of the struggle of the Gentile middle class against Jewish merchants in the cities. This perennial struggle caused a steady exodus of Jews from big cities to the country.[15] Perhaps, therefore, some took a further step and left the commonwealth altogether.

The main destinations of the Jewish emigrants from Poland in this period were the Germanies in the west and the Hapsburg monarchy (Austria, Bohemia, and Moravia) to the southwest. In Germany they were to be found in Frankfort on the Main, Fulda, and Friedberg in the west, in Danzig and Altona in the north, and as we have seen above, in Frankfort on the Oder in Prussia. In the Hapsburg monarchy, Bohemia was the chief target of emigrants, and Vienna to a lesser degree. The Germanies and Bohemia were the focal points of Polish Jewish emigration during the period. This is attested to by the fact that in 1635 the Council of the Four Lands, worried about an increase in the number of *agunoth* (deserted wives), sent a special official to these two areas to track down men who had left their wives behind in Poland and were not heard of again.[16]

Holland and its colony in Brazil also attracted emigrants. We have seen how one man fled from the vicinity of Lemberg to Amsterdam because of "business troubles." Other immigrants to Amsterdam were printers, who found employment in a recently established printing press.[17] The Polish Jews who reached Brazil were traders; some were there as early as 1637. A few years later one of them fell into the hands of the Inquisition.[18] Undoubtedly they first emigrated to Hol-

22

land and from there went to the colonies. All this makes it very likely that even before 1648 Holland absorbed a considerable number of Polish emigrants.

It is hard to arrive at any accurate estimate of the numbers of Jews who emigrated westward in this period. The 400 or 500 Polish Jews living in Danzig cannot serve as an example for other regions. After all, this port city was on the border, and its decisive role in Poland's international trade created very favorable conditions for Jewish immigration. And yet we must assume that the number of Jews who left Poland during the first half of the seventeenth century was large. The merchants who settled in Danzig probably brought their families as well. We have documentary evidence of this for those who settled in Vienna.[19] The same can also be assumed of the immigrants who were permitted to settle in Frankfort on the Oder. But the strongest indication that they came in considerable numbers is the fact that the nickname Pollack was current both in the Germanies and in the Hapsburg monarchy.

The number of immigrants arriving without families was considerable, too. In this category belong many teachers, some of whom returned to Poland after accumulating earnings in the West. This was often the case in the eighteenth century, and there is no reason to think it was different in the seventeenth.[20] Still, a large number of immigrants who arrived without families did stay permanently in the new country. Had their number not been large, the Council of the Four Lands would not have sent a messenger to look for them in Germany and Bohemia.

Practically all immigrants went west with the intention of staying permanently. We find among them persons who married in the new country, and we have evidence that many actually remained in the West to the end of their lives. In many cases their children, too, stayed in the new country until their deaths.[21] The immigrants from Poland thus became an integral part of the Jewish population in the Western World during the first part of the seventeenth century. In some cities, such as Frankfort on the Oder and Altona, the arrival of the immigrants from Eastern Europe actually coincided with the establishment of their Jewish communities.

The Years 1648-1660 and After

I

Dᴜʀɪɴɢ the years of the Cossack uprising and the Muscovite-Swedish invasion, emigration became an issue of much wider scope than hitherto. The chronicles that describe the tribulations of the years 1648-1660 make it clear that masses of Jews who lived in the areas affected by the unrest had to leave their homes to save their lives.[1] This is attested to by other sources as well. A Yiddish poem, *Die Beschreibung fun Ashkenaz un Polack*, written about 1675, tells that because of the wars in Poland, "everybody escaped to [a place] he could [reach]," and implies that the Polish Jews who reached Germany considered themselves war refugees.[2] The sources also describe the fate of individual families. In 1648 a sister of Menahem Mendel Krochmal, chief rabbi of Moravia, fled with her three children from Chelm to her brother in Nikolsburg.[3] A certain scholar fled in the same year from Krzemieniec in Volhynia to Kalisz in western Poland.[4] Many similar cases are recorded in the sources.

In general, the Jews of the Ukraine did not flee their homes until the actual arrival of the Cossacks.[5] But when the Muscovites and Swedes began to invade the country, the migratory movement started at once. Obviously, the experience of 1648 made the people alert to danger. When the Swedes began to march on Cracow, many Jews there immediately fled to Silesia and Moravia.[6] Jews in the vicinity of Posen did not wait even that long. In August 1655 about a thousand requested permission from the Austrian emperor to enter Silesia.[7] That fall we find a group of refugees from Lithuania going to the Baltic port city of Memel in the territory of Prussia.[8] In all the parts of the Polish commonwealth invaded by the Muscovites and Swedes, Jews attempted to reach the nearest border and escape to neighboring countries in the West.

The wars of the 1640s and 1650s brought about a basic deterioration in the political and social conditions of the Polish-Lithuanian commonwealth. Political unrest was growing, and with it the oppression of the Jewish population. A wave of blood accusations swept the northwestern part of the country, and whole Jewish communities had to flee across the border.[9] The deterioration in the general situation of Poland's Jews can be seen in a report given by Tobias the Physician, a native of Metz. In the 1670s he went to settle in Poland, where many of his relatives lived. However, when he "saw the poverty, the oppression, the wars in that land, and the many and frequent troubles," he returned to the West.[10] The situation that Tobias found explains why the migratory drive of the Polish Jews continued to rise even after the riots and invasions had ended.

The favorable economic climate in Western Europe was a sharp contrast to the troubled conditions in Poland. Almost all over Europe favorable opportunities developed for Jewish peddlers. At this time throughout the Germanies court-Jews emerged as bankers to ruling princes and as suppliers of armies. Court-Jews lived in great affluence, and with them the whole Jewish population was raising its standard of living.[11]

Court-Jews felt a need for philanthropic activities. They established Hebrew printing presses and gave financial support to many scholars. Some of them founded *Klausen*, private houses of study for the Talmudic scholars they supported. Even a Portuguese court-Jew of the duke of Mecklenburg had a resident scholar from Poland as a study companion in his Schwerin home.[12] Many scholars from Poland took advantage of similar opportunities and became residents of various *Klausen.*

However, the greatest opportunities scholars from Poland encountered in Germany were in their professional fields. For example, a certain teacher from Poland accumulated a handsome sum of money in two towns in Holland in just eighteen months.[13] *Die Beschreibung fun Ashkenaz un Polack* emphatically states that whenever Jews in Germany needed rabbis or cantors, they had to bring them from Poland. There was an even greater demand for *melamdim* (teachers), without whom German Jewry would have been in a state of total ignorance.[14]

The fact that some Polish Jews had relatives who had settled in the West in an earlier period was another stimulus to emigration. The sister of the chief rabbi of Moravia who fled with her children to Nikolsburg in 1648 surely was not an exception. In addition, more easily available information about western countries helped to dispel the usual fear of the unknown. In 1650 the Great Elector gave permission to Jewish merchants from Poland to do business in the entire march of Brandenburg. In fact, throughout the second half of the century Jewish merchants from Poland enjoyed governmental support in their business endeavors in all Prussian territories.[15] This prolonged period of business activity in Germany gave many Jews from Poland ample opportunity to become closely acquainted with the country. The Leipzig fairs, a frequent meeting place between Jews from the Polish commonwealth and western countries, played a major role.[16]

Another way of becoming acquainted with Western Europe was available to scholars. Many rabbinic authors from Poland visited Germany and Holland to arrange for the printing of their works by the excellent new Hebrew presses and to obtain financial support to defray publishing expenses. One is inclined to think that often the printing of a book was merely an excuse, while the real purpose of the trip was to look for a rabbinic position. Abraham Lisker, who served as

a rabbi in several Lithuanian towns, is a good example. He
went to Hanover to ask the philanthropist Leffmann Behrens
to support the publication of his book. His daughter then married a close relative of Leffmann and remained in Germany.
Lisker, too, stayed in Hanover until his death in 1684.[17]

All these factors created an atmosphere of emigration
among Poland's Jews. The strong desire to leave Poland can
be seen in an event of the year 1656. That fall a number of
refugees from Poland were staying in the vicinity of Hamburg. It seems they were not tolerated by the local population,
and therefore the Sephardic community of Hamburg provided them with boats to go elsewhere.[18] The possibility of
returning to Poland was not even discussed.

Two contemporary books aided wanderers and can be
considered emigrants' literature. Both were written by emigrants from Poland who had traveled around Europe exten-
sively. Nathan Hanover, also the author of *Abyss of Despair*,
entitled his book, a dictionary published in Prague in 1660,
Safah Verurah (Pure Language), from Zephaniah 3: 9. It is
divided into 19 sections, each listing Hebrew words from
different areas of life with their translation into German, Italian, and Latin. A new edition was published in Amsterdam
in 1701, which was also prepared by an emigrant from Poland, who failed to mention the name of the original author
and added a French translation of the vocabulary. On the
title page the book states it should be of use to "women and
men . . . teachers and merchants, [and] the uneducated who
go to other states and other lands."[19] The fact that it in-
cludes a Latin vocabulary indicates it was not originally
written for the exclusive use of emigrants, but also for students who wished to learn that classical language. However,
the German vocabulary was of practical use to emigrants to
the Germanies.

The second book emigrants used was *Massekheth Derekh
Erez* by Shabethay Bass, who gained fame as the first Jewish
bibliographer. It was published in Yiddish in Amsterdam in
1680, as a pocket-size book and is divided into three parts:

the first contains prayers for travelers to be offered on different occasions; the second describes the currencies used in various places; and the third gives information about traveling conditions in most European countries.[20] The booklet was written primarily for traveling merchants, but it also contains sections of a less practical nature, such as descriptions of coins current in biblical times and instructions for travel in Spain, a country then seldom visited by Jewish merchants. However, because it was in Yiddish and described travel conditions prevalent in those parts of the West which were the main destinations of Jewish emigrants from Poland, its usefulness to them was considerable. Shabethay admits he derived some of his material from wanderers, who in turn had obtained it from guidebooks in use in Poland and Lithuania. This indicates that emigrant literature had a wide scope in Poland and Lithuania and that it aided emigrants in their journeys.

The migratory movement was encouraged further by the friendly attitude of Jews in western countries toward emigrants. Nathan Hanover makes the general statement that refugees were given generous aid everywhere, but "especially in Germany they [German Jews] did more than they could."[21] Glückel of Hameln relates that when refugees from Vilna arrived in Hamburg, her father took ten into his house, though some had contagious diseases.[22] It is safe to assume other Jews acted likewise.

The attitude of Jewish communal institutions toward refugees was equally benevolent. When large groups arrived in Lübeck on their way to Altona in the spring of 1656 the Sephardim of Hamburg were asked to aid them. The latter immediately allocated a certain amount as an initial contribution, and called a mass meeting to make an appeal for the refugees. That fall they also helped to defray the traveling expenses of a group of refugees that had been staying in the vicinity of the city but could not remain there.[23] A similar attitude toward refugees was manifested by the Sephardim of Amsterdam. They founded a society, Zeh Sha'ar Hashamayim

("This is the Gate of Heaven," Genesis 28: 17), to provide food and clothing for refugees. When in 1656 the influx of immigrants to Amsterdam became overwhelming and it was necessary to send about 170 to Germany, the Sephardim paid the costs of the passage.[24] These allocations for traveling expenses were made by the Sephardim of Hamburg and Amsterdam in addition to the aid they extended to refugees who stayed on. The manner in which rich Sephardim in Amsterdam aided them was remarkable. They took many into their homes, generously provided them with food and clothing, and gave each one some money.[25] Energetic actions in favor of refugees were taken by smaller communities as well. For example, in Wallerstein in 1656, when a certain Jew refused to pay his contribution for the wanderers, the communal authorities threatened to excommunicate him that very evening if he did not pay.[26]

A lone exception was Frankfort on the Main, where the Jewish community refused to accept a group of Polish refugees. The Frankfort Jews feared not only the resentment of their Gentile neighbors, but also possible business competitors. The refugees in turn resented this attitude, and even the few (probably scholars) the Frankfort Jews were ready to admit refused to remain. The whole group moved on to another place.[27]

II

A new willingness of certain western governments to admit Jews also encouraged immigration from Eastern Europe. During the Thirty Years' War the pressure of events caused some states and cities to ignore the laws prohibiting the admission of Jews. This tendency grew even stronger after the war. Whenever officials of a state looked for a remedy to the ills caused by the war, they invariably concluded their territory should be opened to Jewish immigrants. It was hoped they would revive commerce and that their tax payments would refill empty treasuries. Economists, too, began to advocate a friendly attitude toward immigrants.[28]

Frederick William of Brandenburg and Prussia, the Great Elector (1640-1688), was genuinely interested in attracting Jewish settlers. While still crown prince, he spent the years 1634-1638 in Holland, where he observed how much the power of a state depended on its maritime trade. He also saw that Dutch Jews played an important role in the country's foreign trade. Consequently, when he ascended the throne he began to admit Jewish immigrants, convinced that their endeavors would strengthen the economy of his expanding monarchy. It was a happy coincidence that when Lithuanian Jewish refugees from the Muscovite-Swedish War were knocking at the gates of East Prussia, this province was already under his control. By and large he remained steadfast in his pro-Jewish policy. He successfully insisted that *Receptio Judeorum* was a right of the prince, and this rendered the opposition of the population to Jewish immigration less effective. In 1672 when he was asked to expel the Jews from one of his territories, the Great Elector told the petitioners the Jews were very useful to the country and he was satisfied to see them settle in its various provinces.[29]

A friendly attitude toward Jewish immigrants was not universal in the Germanies. The diversity of conditions from place to place and the varying personal attitudes of the princes concerning Jews resulted in a complex situation. In Mayence, for example, an order prohibiting the admission of alien Jews was issued in 1662. About ten years later another order decreed a reduction in the number of Jewish families permitted to dwell in the territory. A tendency to decrease the number of Jews became noticeable in Bamberg in the 1680s. The same happened in Prague, where repeated attempts were made during the last twenty years of the century to limit the size of the Jewish population. A truly hostile attitude toward Jewish immigrants was prevalent in the duchy of Hanover. In the years 1685-1700 no less than six decrees against *Betteljuden* were issued, each one more cruel than the preceding one.[30]

The states that manifested an unfriendly attitude toward Jewish immigrants were, however, in the minority. In most regions of the Germanies, Jews were tolerated or even welcomed. Besides the economic interests of the various states, a feeling of compassion for refugees helped to create the friendly climate they encountered in the West. Many government officials who dealt with the Jewish problem developed a sympathetic attitude toward Jews. In 1649 when a certain Jew petitioned the government of Brandenburg for permission to settle in Dinslaken, he indicated in his letter that he had become impoverished because of the Cossack riots. The fact that he saw fit to state his plight shows that sympathetic consideration could be expected from officialdom. A large group of Jews, who asked for the emperor's permission to enter Silesia in 1656, appealed to his compassion. Human sympathy, we may assume, was responsible for the fact that when some Polish Jews crossed the border to Prussia in 1658 and could not earn their livelihood as merchants, they were permitted to work as farmhands.[31]

Pity, too, induced various states to reduce the amount of *Leibzoll* (body tax) incoming Jews had to pay. In 1662 the duchy of Ansbach, for example, reduced the *Leibzoll* for *Betteljuden*, except those who coupled peddling with begging, and destitute Jews were freed from it altogether. In Wallerstein the tax was reduced by 20 percent as early as 1651. The decree mentioned explicitly that the reduction applied to *Betteljuden* from Poland and other countries. In a list of Jews who obtained passports to travel from England to Holland in the years 1689-1696, several by the name of Pollack are described as "poor Jews." In England, too, poor Jews from Poland were treated with consideration and were able to obtain traveling papers.[32]

III

The conditions prevailing in the Polish commonwealth and in the western countries, as described above, were the main factors that caused the migratory movement to become a major phenomenon in the life of Eastern European

32

Jewry throughout the second half of the seventeenth century. The migratory drive was not of equal intensity in all parts of the commonwealth. The sources show beyond doubt that in the provinces immediately bordering on western countries the movement was stronger than in the central and eastern regions. A Prussian document of 1648 explicitly mentions Polish Jews who lived near the border and crossed to the Prussian side. It literally calls them *Grenzjuden* (border Jews).[33] Obviously, the proximity of the border was a major factor in the migratory drive.

This is probably the reason why refugees from the Cossack riots of 1648 in the Ukraine appeared in Western Europe in much smaller numbers than those who escaped as a result of the Muscovite-Swedish invasion of 1654-1658. The refugees of 1648 left the Ukraine in large groups; at times entire communities fled as a whole. Nathan Hanover's description of how his own community of Zaslaw escaped is evidence of this.[34] However, on their way westward the groups dissolved, and their members dispersed throughout the Polish commonwealth. They are found in Lemberg, Lublin, Zamosc, Cracow, and elsewhere.[35] An example of this development is the scholar from Krzemieniec mentioned above, who settled in Kalisz and whose family later spread to several towns in western Poland. Those Ukrainian refugees, however, who did leave Poland for Western Europe usually did so singly. We find sole refugees from the Ukraine in many places in the West; for example, a young scholar in Holleschau, Moravia; a man from Perejaslaw, who lived in Deutz in western Germany; and Rabbi Moses of Narol, who became rabbi of Metz.[36] Evidence of refugees from the Ukraine of the years 1648-1649 who reached Western Europe in groups does not seem to exist. Many a time historians have written of groups of refugees from the Cossack riots in Western Europe. However, they invariably based their descriptions on sources that in reality refer to refugees from the Muscovite-Swedish invasion of the 1650s.[37]

The only country where groups of refugees from Poland

did arrive in 1648-1649 was Moravia. A census of the permanent Jewish inhabitants taken in various Moravian towns in 1657 revealed the presence of a relatively large number of people whose surname was Pollack.[38] Had they been refugees of 1655-1656, their names probably would not have been included in these lists of permanent inhabitants. Additional proof is found in the fact that in 1650 the Moravian *Landtag* (diet) resolved to withdraw the permission of residence from all Jews who came after 1618, because "they became too numerous."[39] This act of the diet shows that Polish Jews were already immigrating to Moravia during the Thirty Years' War. But the fact that the law was passed in 1650 indicates that the number of refugees grew considerably in 1648-1649.

Though large groups of refugees entered Moravia already during the uprising of the Cossacks, in other parts of Western Europe we find only single immigrants from the Ukraine.[40] This is mainly attributable to the distance of the Ukraine from the western borders of the Polish commonwealth. But, when the invasions of the Muscovites and Swedes brought down a great calamity on the Jews of Lithuania (near East Prussia) and western Poland (near Brandenburg, Silesia, and Moravia), they crossed the borders in groups. Indeed, even large groups. The sources tell about large groups of refugees arriving in Germany and Holland. Glückel reports that many refugees from Vilna appeared in Hamburg. The minutes book of the Portuguese community of Hamburg also records that in the summer of 1656 "a large group" of refugees, numbering in the hundreds, arrived in that city.[41] In that same year great numbers of refugees went to Vienna, too. The group was so large that the Jewish community there was compelled to ask the community of Venice to assist in their maintenance.[42]

An analysis of the regions and cities the emigrants came from offers additional evidence that the vicinity of the border played a decisive role in the migratory movement. This became clear during the Muscovite-Swedish invasion. The

1626238

more than 1,000 refugees who entered Silesia were all inhabitants of western Poland. The chronicle *Tit Hayawen* reports
that about 100 families fled from Lissa to Germany.[43] The
rabbi of Krotoschin, Menahem Mann ben Moses, tells that he
escaped "with the refugees of the holy community Krotoschin."[44] Similar information comes from Lithuania. Rabbi
Moses Rivkes tells that he and other refugees from Vilna first
fled to Samogitia, close to East Prussia, and from there sailed
to Amsterdam. Other Lithuanian Jews also took boats to Amsterdam, he reports. Additional Lithuanian refugees fled to
the Prussian port city of Memel. In a special order dated 26
October 1656, the Great Elector took them under his protection and gave them the privilege of residing and trading in
East Prussia.[45] From Cracow, close to the borders of Silesia,
Moravia, and Austria, a considerable number of Jews fled
when the Swedes approached the city. Rabbi Abraham
Bochner emigrated to Vienna with his entire yeshivah.
Among the refugees from Cracow were many Ukrainian Jews
who had settled in the city after their escape in 1648 from
the Cossack riots. Now, when they had to flee again, they
crossed the border to the West, because Cracow was com-
paratively close to it.[46]

The vicinity of the border as a factor promoting migration is further shown by the fact that emigrants who left the
Polish commonwealth in the latter decades of the seventeenth century, and cannot be considered war refugees, also
came primarily from regions located on the western border.
Of the five synagogues established by Jews from Poland in
Breslau in the second half of the century, three were founded
by Jews from western Poland. The statutes of the Jewish
community of Auras, a town near Breslau, required that
the *Haftorah* be read according to the order followed in
Lissa. Obviously, this community was founded by immigrants from Lissa.[47] In the Hebrew printing presses established at that time in the Germanies and Amsterdam, we
find immigrant proofreaders, mostly from western Poland.
Four of the six proofreaders of the Talmud published in 1696

in Frankfort on the Oder were from western Poland. The Proops printing press in Amsterdam was established by a family from Posen.[48]

Among the rabbis and nonprofessional scholars who arrived from Poland in Western Europe late in the century, were immigrants from western Poland and Lithuania. For example, immigrant scholars who settled in Hanover came from Posen, Lissa, and Meseritsch in western Poland, and from Kejdany in Samogitia, while we find only one scholar from Lublin. Other immigrant rabbis in Germany came from Cracow. In London, too, we find in 1662 a rabbi who grew up in Cracow and studied in a yeshivah there.[49]

The same holds true for emigrants who were not scholars. Sometime between 1670 and 1680 four Jews were lost at sea. Of their four widows, three lived in Samogitia. Obviously, the travelers were Lithuanians.[50] At the close of the century the stream of emigrants from Lithuania to London also increased,[51] and there were many immigrants from western Poland in the territories of the Brandenburg-Prussian state. Of 52 Jewish families that lived in the province of Pomerania in 1700, 17 had migrated from western Poland. At that time immigrants from Posen and Kalisz also lived in Frankfort on the Oder, Dessau, and Halberstadt.[52] In 1681 we find a Jew from Kalisz in a small town in Bavaria.[53] There were, of course, exceptions. It sometimes happened that people who lived close to one border emigrated by way of a more distant border. For instance, prominent rabbis of Vilna, Ephraim Hakohen, author of *Sha'ar Efrayim,* and Shabbethai Kohen (the Shakh) first went to central Poland, and then to Moravia. Similarly, we know of three women who fled from Vilna to Nikolsburg in Moravia.[54]

The role the vicinity of the border played in the migratory movement is finally attested to by our sample list of some 140 Polish emigrants of the second half of the seventeenth century: 88 (62 percent) came from regions near the western borders of the commonwealth, and only 52 (38 percent) from other areas. Of the 88 emigrants, 48 were from western Poland, 22 from Cracow and vicinity, and 18 from Lithuania. An analysis of a list of 45 emigrants from the interior of Poland shows that 17 came from the southeast (now East Galicia), 16 from central regions (between Kielce in the west and Lublin in the east) and 12 from the east (Wolhynia and the Ukraine). Hence various regions of "inner" Poland furnished emigrants in approximately the same proportion as elsewhere. These lists thus confirm the results obtained from the literary and documentary sources at our disposal.[55]

IV

The emigrants who left the Polish commonwealth spread all over Western Europe. We have seen that Jews from western Poland emigrated primarily to the Germanies. A contemporary rabbinic responsum speaks of "all the divorce certificates that are being sent from Germany to the Polish commonwealth."[56] This implies that the Germanies were a major area of Jewish immigration from Poland. Large numbers of these immigrants settled in Brandenburg-Prussia because of its proximity to Poland and the friendly attitude of the Great Elector. To be sure, in 1657 he ordered the immigration of Polish Jews to East Prussia stopped because there were already "too many" and there was an epidemic in Poland. Still, the number of immigrants from Poland grew, and in 1663 the elector ordered them to be banished "because many of them have arrived and they keep on arriving daily in ever growing numbers."[57] There is no record that this order of expulsion was ever carried out. A review of the whole attitude of the Great Elector toward immigrants from Poland would suggest he issued these orders only to appease opponents of Jewish immigration. It is also possible that the tide of immigration could not be stopped because it was stronger than administrative orders. Indeed, up to the end of the century and even until the death of Frederick I in 1713, an uninterrupted stream of Jewish immigrants was moving to all parts of the Prussian state.[58] Of a sample list of about 90 immigrants who entered the Germanies during the second half of the seventeenth century, more than 40 percent settled in the Prussian monarchy. We find them throughout the eastern and western provinces of the state. Aside from East Prussia, according to Selma Stern, Berlin was the main destination of the Polish immigrants. Glückel reports that one of her sons, who at that time lived in Berlin, had business dealings with "Pollacken."[59]

Immigrants from Poland also appeared in this period in the electorate of Saxony and the duchy of Anhalt. In Saxony their number was small because of the strong opposition of the citizenry. But there is no doubt that Polish Jews lived in the electorate before 1700; in 1708 an order was issued to expel them.[60] The number of Polish Jews in the duchy of Anhalt was larger. After the duke admitted some of them to Dessau in 1678, more and more Polish Jews settled there, among them the ancestors of Moses Mendelssohn. Still more Polish Jews settled in the town when a Hebrew printing press was established there in 1694 by a philanthropist, a son of Polish immigrants. Others settled in Bernburg, in the same duchy.[61]

The immigration of Polish Jews to northern Germany was quite large. We have described above how boats with refugees from the Muscovite-Swedish invasion arrived in Hamburg and Altona. Jacob Emden tells that the *Klaus* established by his father in Altona "was joined by famous scholars and rabbis from Poland and Lithuania." In Moisling, which was under Danish control, a Jewish community was established by immigrants who had come from at least five towns in Poland. Moreover, Polish Jews also succeeded in settling in the nearby Hanseatic city of Lübeck. To be sure, in 1699 an order was issued to expel them, but the citizenry continued to complain that Jews kept coming by land and sea from Poland, Kurland, and Prussia. Jews of the lower classes likewise streamed into northern Germany. From 1685 to

1700 the state of Hanover issued no less than six rigid orders against wandering Jews. Refugees from the Muscovite-Swedish invasion were also found in Emden, in northwestern Germany.[62] The important place that northern Germany occupied on the migration map of the Eastern European Jews is further confirmed by the sample list of emigrants we have collected. About 20 percent of the 90 emigrants to the Germanies settled in northern cities.

Fewer Polish Jews emigrated to western Germany than to Prussia and the north. Of the many refugees who arrived in Amsterdam in 1656, some left for western Germany: about 130 refugees went to Mayence and about 40 to Deutz. Later, too, Polish Jews immigrated to this area. The sample list of emigrants shows that about 15 percent settled in various places in western Germany: in cities along the Rhine, in the provinces of Baden, in Hesse, and in Frankfort on the Main.[63] In today's Bavaria, the city of Fürth was the main destination of immigrants from Poland. But we find them in other towns as well; for example, in Ansbach, Wallerstein, and Öttingen. In 1681 a Jew from Kalisz lived in the little town of Dennenlohe. A convert from Cracow lived in 1661 in Nuremberg. That there was a constant movement of Polish Jews into Bavaria is shown by the fact that of the 12 foreign Jews who passed the town of Lauingen in 1665, 4 were from Poland.[64] In the list of 90 emigrants who made their home in the Germanies, we find about 20 had settled in Bavaria, mostly in Fürth.

In the Hapsburg monarchy Moravia was the main province into which Polish Jews moved during the years 1648-1657. Between 1657 and 1677 we find Polish immigrants in at least 16 towns and cities there. It seems that the number who immigrated to Bohemia was much smaller. Nathan Hanover mentions Bohemia in his *Abyss of Despair* as one of the countries refugees of 1648-1649 went to. The petition Jews of western Poland submitted to the emperor in 1656 explicitly mentioned Bohemia as a province to which they wished to go. Yet the number of immigrants who did go to Bohemia was relatively small. They preferred Moravia, both because it was closer to the Polish border and because it offered better economic opportunities. In *Megillath Sefer* Jacob Emden lists the Germanies and Moravia, but not Bohemia, as places where the rabbis of Vilna sought refuge. Contemporary rabbinic literature, too, contains information about emigration from Poland mainly to Moravia, but rarely to Bohemia. We also know that great efforts were made to limit the Jewish population in Prague during the last twenty years of the century. Nevertheless, a certain number of Polish Jews did go to Prague in 1648-1649.[65]

Silesia was also a part of the Hapsburg monarchy. It was natural for a region where Polish was still spoken to attract immigrants from the commonwealth. Even after the expulsion of 1582 Jews were permitted to reside in the cities of Glogau and Zülz. During the Thirty Years' War they began to be tacitly admitted to many other towns and cities.[66] We have seen that a large number of Jews from western Poland entered Silesia at the time of the Swedish invasion. According to their representatives, most of these refugees had returned to Poland by 1660. We have proof, however, that others remained in Silesia. Some Jews of Cracow also fled to Silesia when the Swedes approached the old Polish capital. There is evidence that Polish Jews and their families arrived in Silesia later in the century, too. They settled in various places, including the old communities of Glogau and Zülz.[67] Gradually a Jewish community grew up in Breslau, the capital of Silesia, mainly as a result of immigration from Poland. To be sure, the first few Jews who gained permission to settle in Breslau were coiners from Bohemia. A Jewish community, however, was established there in connection with Breslau's annual fair. A list of Jewish merchants who came to the fair in 1696 shows that 60 percent were from Poland. Most of them usually returned to Poland after the fair. There were, however, Jews who went to Breslau to make it their home. The tailor Kathri'el, who came from Lithuania with his wife and child, certainly was not a visitor to the fair but an immigrant. The Polish shoemaker Me'ir Jacob, who was denied admission to Breslau when it became known that he had been expelled from Prague, was also such an immigrant. Besides these "illegal" immigrants, a number of Polish Jews were officially permitted to reside in Breslau. They were called *Schamessen* (attendants) and served as business agents for foreign Jewish merchants in the periods between the fairs. Such an agent is first mentioned in a document of 1673. Of the ten *Schamessen* who lived in Breslau in 1696, six were from Poland. The *Schamessen*, their families, and Jews in their service became the true founders of the Jewish community of Breslau. The rise of the Polish Jewish settlement there is amply manifested by the five synagogues established before the end of the seventeenth century by immigrants from Kalisz, Krotoschin, Lemberg, Lissa, and Volhynia. That these synagogues were not just temporary establishments for visitors to the fair is shown by the fact that one was still in existence recently.[68]

We have seen that in 1656 a sizable number of Polish Jews fled to Vienna, mainly from Cracow. Somewhat later we find houseowners whose names indicate their Polish origin. Several rabbis from Poland also lived there. The expulsion of 1670 stopped Jewish immigration, but at the end of the century a small number of Polish Jews again lived in Vienna.[69]

Although Holland in general, and especially Amsterdam, was a major destination of refugees from the Ukraine, some having arrived as early as 1648, the Lithuanian refugees of 1656 were far more numerous. Various sources report the sailing of many refugees from Memel and other Baltic ports to Holland. So many arrived on the island of Texel in northern Holland and in Amsterdam that it was necessary to send some of them to western Germany. From Amsterdam many Polish Jews spread out to neighboring towns. At the end of the century large numbers of poor Jews arrived in Amsterdam; many were emigrants from Poland. Many Polish refugees settled in Rotterdam and in The Hague, where there had been no Jewish community before their arrival. Some also settled in the province of Overijssel. In the city of Groningen they formed a Jewish proletariat resembling Amsterdam's. In Holland, as in Moravia, Jewish immigrants from Poland spread all over the country.[70]

The number of Jewish emigrants from Poland who reached France in that period was not large. Some refugees of the years 1648-1656, however, did settle there. A good example is Rabbi Moses of Narol, who went to Germany in 1648 and from there proceeded to Metz. It seems that in the last decade of the century, Polish Jewish immigration to France increased. To begin with, in that decade about 800 poor Jewish families went to Alsace. It is safe to assume that among them were Jews from Poland, as was always the case with poor wandering Jews. Further evidence of migration to France is the fact that the second edition of the dictionary *Safah Verurah*, published for emigrants in 1701, contains a French vocabulary. Here and there in France we find rabbis of Polish origin, such as Aron Lwow, a native of Lemberg who by the end of the century was a rabbi in Alsace, and Abraham Liptsis, who in 1677 was rabbi in Isle-sur-Sorg in the south.[71]

A small group of Polish immigrants settled in Switzerland in this period. In 1684 one Joachim Pollag lived in Mammern, in the canton of Thurgau. We find numerous Pollags in Endingen, in the canton of Aargau, during the first half of the eighteenth century; at least one of their ancestors already lived there in 1689.[72]

It is questionable whether a boat with Jewish refugees from Poland arrived in London in 1648, as asserted by Lucien Wolf. Moreover, it seems that even during the years 1655-1657, when many boatloads of Lithuanian Jews did leave for the West, few went to England in comparison with the many who sailed for Germany and Holland. Polish immigrants probably shunned England because the Ashkenazic element in English Jewry was still very small. Before the century closed, however, a stream of Polish and Lithuanian Jews began to move to England. Their number continued to grow, and the name Pollack became quite common. Before the end of the century a few Polish Jews also settled in Glückstadt, the port city on the German Sea founded and controlled by Denmark.[73]

V

An analysis of the occupations of Polish emigrants reveals they were mainly communal functionaries, scholars, and merchants. According to our sample list, about half of them were rabbis, teachers, cantors, authors, and proofreaders. The professional intelligentsia were eager to emigrate because of the opportunities open to them in the West. In addition, the Jewish communities and their leaders had a friendlier attitude toward this type of immigrant than toward the ordinary man.[74] We find in the sources much information about Polish rabbis who settled in all parts of the Germanies, and in Austria, Moravia, France, Holland, and England.[75] The similarity between the Polish order of prayer and the Ashkenazic rite also made it possible for many cantors to obtain positions in the West. *Die Beschreibung fun Ashkenaz un Polack*, which stresses German Jewry's need for Polish *melamdim* (teachers), relates that many actually did immigrate to the West. Many proofreaders from Poland worked for Hebrew printing presses in Silesia, Germany and Holland.[76] As we have seen, quite a number of authors went to Western Europe to publish their works; equally numerous were the resident scholars in the *Klausen* established by magnanimous supporters of learning.[77]

Merchants, both peddlers and businessmen, were another important group of emigrants. From the Yiddish poem just mentioned, it is evident that *pakntreger* (ambulant merchants) were a very large group among the immigrants in the Germanies. Various sources, including Glückel's *Memoirs*, mention immigrants from Poland who were businessmen. An interesting example is Simon Wolf of Vilna, a wealthy Jew of aristocratic origin, who fled to Germany with his family. In a short time the business enterprises of the family spread widely and reached the princely courts. Some of Wolf's relatives settled in Dessau, where they established factories and conducted business activities on a large scale. Among the Jewish merchants attending the Leipzig fairs, we find about twenty named Pollack who resided in the Germanies and the Hapsburg monarchy. The immigrants among the visitors to the fairs probably were even more numerous, since many who bore names other than Pollack cannot be identified as from Poland. In Holland, too, we find immigrants prominent in the business world. Between 1680 and 1700 a considerable number were stockholders of the Dutch East India Company.[78] Many immigrants were peddlers and some earned their livelihood as employees of wealthy Sephardic merchants.[79]

VI

In addition to the various categories of immigrants described above, wandering Jews, too, tried to penetrate the countries of the West. After the calamity of the years 1648-1658, they were seen more frequently everywhere, but appeared mostly in localities which already had Jewish populations. A certain number of families, especially those with pregnant women, were usually admitted into the towns. In some towns, when a child was born to an itinerant Jew, the family was permitted to reside there permanently. The author of *Die Beschreibung fun Ashkenaz un Polack*, who speaks explicitly of the arrival of Polish *Betteljuden* in the Germanies, reports that they made efforts to settle permanently in towns they "liked." No doubt, most of them were not beggars, but rather people who wanted to obtain the right of settlement.[80] An official document of one government refers to itinerant Jews "from Poland and other countries." That

Betteljuden from Poland were mentioned specifically suggests they were the largest group. In England, too, some Polish Jews were officially designated by the authorities as "poor men."[81]

When their numbers began to rise, wandering Jews became a problem to both the governments and the Jewish communities. The attitude of the governments became generally less friendly than hitherto. On the other hand, the Jewish communities often tried to help itinerant Jews. A good example of such assistance is the special tax imposed by the community of Wallerstein in 1656 for the support of *Betteljuden*, and the drastic measures taken to collect the tax.[82] The Yiddish poem also reports that extensive aid was given to refugee wanderers. There is no doubt that without the aid German Jewry extended to the wanderers, their sojourn in Germany would have been impossible.

The hardships of wandering and the refusal of most governments to grant them rights of settlement drove some *Betteljuden* to conversion or crime. When a famous golden plate was stolen from the altar of a monastery in Lüneburg in northern Germany in 1698, the arrest of the culprits revealed that about half of them were Jews from Poland, either converted to Christianity or alienated from Judaism.[83]

VII

The only aspect of the migratory movement that seems to elude description is the actual number of Jews who left their homes for the West. Statistical data do not exist, and the available sources tell only part of the story. All that can be safely said is that whenever we try to arrive at definite numbers, they are inevitably smaller than the number of people who actually emigrated. The surname Pollack by which arrivals from Poland were often known was not the only name used by emigrants.[84] *Schutzbriefe* (patents granting right of residence) for new arrivals frequently fail to mention the places of origin of their holders. In the case of Prussia, this is true of most *Schutzbriefe.*[85]

All this makes it impossible to chart the statistics of emigration in those times. We must be satisfied with a general discussion of the problem which may give us at least some idea of the dimensions of the migratory movement. The available information on individual emigrants indicates that in most cases they left for the West with their families.[86] This means that each emigrant's name found in the sources represents a group of five or six persons. We also know that some of the emigrants were converted to Christianity after they left Poland.[87] Consequently, we may assume the number of emigrants was actually larger than that found in the Jewish communities in the West. With regard to certain categories of immigrants, as for example *melamdim*, the sources explicitly say "many Poles" were among them.[88] Furthermore, we have to consider the fact that the wave of blood accusations which swept Poland at that time resulted in the flight of entire communities to the West. Statements of government circles in the Germanies linking the rapid growth of the Jewish population to immigration from Poland may well be true.[89]

Only for certain localities can we estimate the proportion of immigrants in the general Jewish population. In Moravia, where lists of the Jewish inhabitants in many towns have been preserved, we find that between 10 and 15 percent had surnames indicating Polish origin.[90] If we also take into account that many immigrants had "neutral" names, we may safely assume that around 1675 immigrants from Poland constituted about 20 percent of Moravia's total Jewish population. Around the same time the Polish arrivals in Amsterdam also numbered between 15 and 20 percent of the total Jewish population. When the community of Polish Jews there demanded a share in the proceeds of the Ashkenazic *shehitah* (ritual slaughter), the municipality recognized its right to 20 percent of the income. The Polish community, however, believed its share should be larger.[91] This argument shows that it was commonly known that at least one fifth of Amster-

dam's Ashkenazim came from Poland. If we further consider
the fact that in the 1670s the Ashkenazic population was
twice as large as the Sephardic, we may conclude immigrants
from Poland constituted between 13 and 15 percent of the
total Jewish population.[92] A reliable source relates that in
1671 the Polish Jewish community in Amsterdam numbered
70 families, or between 350 and 400 souls.[93] We have also
seen that other regions and cities in Holland had considerable numbers of refugees from Poland. As their relative
strength within the Jewish communities likewise seems to
have been sizable, we may assume Polish immigrants in Holland constituted from 10 to 15 percent of the total Jewish population. It is impossible to conclude whether the percentage
of Polish immigrants was similar in the entire area of immigration in the West.

VIII

More information is available about the efforts of emigrants to establish themselves in their new countries and to
become an integral part of the local Jewish populations. To
begin with, very few emigrants returned to Poland, and if
they did, their families often remained in the West. For example, the children of Aaron Kaidanover stayed on in Silesia
and Germany after he returned to Poland to serve as a rabbi
in Cracow.[94] The fact that many divorce certificates were
sent from Germany to Poland shows that many men, who for
some reason had emigrated without their families, chose not
to return to Poland.[95] Occasionally immigrant families in the
West can be traced through several generations; such information is available from the Germanies, Silesia, Moravia,
Austria, and Holland.[96]

Marriage between members of immigrant families and
native Jews was an important step in the process of integration. Although the author of *Die Beschreibung fun Ashkenaz
un Pollack* complains that German Jews were reluctant to

marry immigrants from Poland, even if they were *benei Torah* (scholars), the sources nevertheless record many marriages between Polish and German Jews. Glückel, a reliable witness in these matters, mentions several such marriages. We also possess detailed information about children of immigrant rabbis who married into native families, at times very wealthy families.[97]

Knowledge of the languages spoken in western countries gradually spread among the immigrants. No doubt, the multilingual dictionary *Safah Verurah*, especially its second edition (1701), helped emigrants who went to Germany and France. As far as Dutch is concerned, we know that immigrants were already using it in the 1670s. With regard to German, it is worth noting that Hartog Leo, a son of the Torah scribe Aryeh Löb who immigrated to Germany from Posen, became a German poet.[98]

Nevertheless, the relationships between newcomers and native Jews were tense, as is always the case in times of large scale immigration. As new immigrants and *Betteljuden* followed the refugees of the years 1648-1658, it became evident that the migration of East European Jews was not a passing event but rather a continuous movement. The Jews of the West found fault with their brethren from Poland, especially disliking their long garments. For their part, immigrants argued that the Jews of the West did not extend a friendly welcome.[99] It is obvious that the tension between the two groups had grown to such proportions that the immigrants even forgot the brotherly reception given the refugees in 1656. In Amsterdam they developed a tendency toward separatism and attempted to establish an independent Polish *qehillah* (religious community). The Jews from Poland who immigrated to Amsterdam prior to 1656 naturally joined the Ashkenazic community. However, when large groups of Lithuanian Jews arrived in 1656, friction developed, and in 1660 the refugees established a separate *qehillah* that worshipped according to the Lithuanian order of prayer. The separatism of the newcomers went so far as to induce them to solicit the support of the Council of the Four Lands in their quarrel with the Ashkenazic community. It seems that after the Polish-Lithuanian *qehillah* was dissolved by government order, its members continued to pray in their separate synagogue.[100] To be sure, Polish immigrants also had separate synagogues in other places, such as Breslau and Auras. These synagogues, however, were not established as a result of separatist tendencies, but because immigrants from Poland founded the new Jewish communities in these localities.

In other communities separatism did not develop. No information is available about friction between immigrant and native Jews in places like Dessau and Moisling, where both groups settled simultaneously.[101] In the Hague, where the Jewish community was founded by immigrants from Poland, the Sephardim who arrived later were permitted to bury their dead in the "Polish" cemetery.[102]

Almost everywhere in the West we find immigrants from Poland active in the leadership of Jewish communities and their institutions. In Berlin, for example, a member of the Wulff family of Vilna was an important leader. An immigrant teacher who became wealthy played a similar role in Hildesheim.[103] Immigrants founded burial societies in Berlin and Amsterdam, and willed charitable funds to their communities.[104] A good example of an immigrant who was active in communal affairs was Shabethay Bass. After he opened his famous printing press in Dyhernfurth in Silesia, he established many religious and charitable institutions for the benefit of the new community.[105]

In the area of Hebrew printing, immigrants from Poland made a major contribution. The famous press opened by the Proops family in Amsterdam was mentioned above. Proofreaders from Poland also worked for Gentile printers in Amsterdam who published Hebrew books. Before the end of the century the Wulff family of Vilna opened a printing press in Dessau which branched out into other cities in central Germany.[106] Printing presses were an important channel for spreading the cultural and religious influence of immigrant rabbis and authors in western countries.

At this point it should be added that the poorer and less educated immigrants fared better in Holland than in the Germanies, where many remained homeless and jobless *Betteljuden.* In Holland, however, we do not find such complete déclassés. Despite the opposition of the authorities, practically all immigrants found work or became ambulant vendors. These poor immigrants established Amsterdam's Jewish proletariat that existed until World War II.[107] Some of them, however, began to ascend the ladder of economic success. The constitution adopted in the 1670s by the Polish-Lithuanian *qehillah* in Amsterdam clearly reflects an economically integrated and prospering society. The sources also offer information about individuals who attained spectacular economic success. Even some *melamdim* became wealthy.[108] In general there is ample information about wealthy immigrants from Poland in the Germanies and Holland, but in most cases it is hard to determine whether they brought their wealth with them or accumulated it after their arrival in the West.[109]

CHAPTER THREE

The First Half of the Eighteenth Century

I

Wᴵᴛʜ the advent of the eighteenth century the migratory movement of Polish Jews to western countries continued to gain strength. A recently published book describing Jewish life in Germany during this period mentions them with considerable frequency.[1] It seems that there was no area of Jewish life in which immigrants were not active in some way. A contemporary Polish Jewish author who went to Germany describes a situation typical of a period of large scale immigration when he speaks of "men who are separated from their wives for long periods of time in distant lands."[2] Another author, who left Poland before 1722, talks about emigrants in the style of the *Midrash*: "From strange land to strange land—this refers to the emigrants from Poland."[3]

The increase in the intensity of the migratory movement was caused by the same factors that drove the Jews of Poland to emigrate in the second half of the seventeenth century. Moreover, all these factors now were much more potent than in the preceding era. The political situation of the Polish commonwealth was very serious. During the first decade of the eighteenth century the country was ravaged by the Great Northern War, which brought a repetition of the atrocities of the Muscovite-Swedish invasion of the 1650s. In the 1730s the Polish commonwealth again became an arena for the armies of the competing pretenders Stanislaw Leszczyński and Augustus III of Saxony. During the half century the two Saxon kings ruled, the commonwealth experienced a state of growing anarchy. The Jewish population was subjected to endless persecution and had to endure a long chain of blood libel trials. This period was justly described by historians as one of the darkest ages in the life of the Jewish people in Eastern Europe.[4] The insecurity of the Jews in Poland is illustrated by the never ceasing attempts of the burgesses of Lublin to expel them from a city in which they had been living for many centuries.[5]

The tragic plight of the Jews of Poland is clearly depicted in the statements of emigrants. Joseph ben Jacob, rabbi of Selyets in Lithuania, reminisced: "I was compelled to leave my home and to become a wanderer [in 1702] because of the rage of the oppressor whose hand was heavy on us . . . the oppression and the catastrophe that came upon us made it impossible for us to live in the country of Poland-Lithuania."[6] The same expression "the rage of the oppressor" is also given as the reason why Rabbi Jacob Joshua, author of *Pene Yehoshu'a,* had to leave the country in 1730.[7] In 1708 a part of the Jewish community of Brody was compelled to flee the city. One of the rabbis, Hirsch Auerbach, who fled to Germany and became a rabbi in Worms, tells that he had to leave "because of the heavy burden of taxes and because of the informers."[8] The plague of informers was widespread and greatly contributed to the lowering of the status of the rabbinate. In addition, *taqifim* (authoritarian individuals) ruled many communities. These were the conditions that made so many rabbis eager to leave their homes and look for positions in western countries.[9] Abraham Meisels, rabbi of Wishnitza in Lithuania, who arrived in Holland at that time, described the tragic situation in his native country in these words: "From a desert I have come, from a land of terror, the land of Poland."[10] That Jews also fled from the armies fighting on Polish territory can be seen in two Prussian documents of 1709 and 1734. They show that the Prussian government permitted wealthy Jewish war refugees to stay in the provinces of Pomerania and Neumark.[11] In addition to the political troubles, poverty and unemployment spread rapidly among the Jews. Statements made by emigrants stress the economic factor was essential in their decision to emigrate. In 1722, for example, a leader of the Jewish community of Minsk emigrated to Altona after having lost all he possessed. An author, a native of Komarno in Galicia, relates in the introduction to his work, published in 1710 in Amsterdam, that "most of the Jews in these lands live in complete poverty; they simply starve." He tells that the serious economic situation caused many *melamdim* (teachers) to emigrate to the West. The famous astronomer Jonathan of Rozan said that the Jewish population of various provinces was completely impoverished in those times. In 1710, he reports, an epidemic broke out in his home town, followed by famine and war, so that "all the wealthy men lost their fortunes and became impoverished." He adds that he was among the victims of these hard times and therefore was forced to emigrate to Frankfort on the Main.[12]

Just as Poland's Jews were sinking politically and economically, their co-religionists in Western Europe were continuing to make use of the new opportunities for economic advancement opened to them in the second half of the seventeenth century. These opportunities were also generally open to the more capable among the immigrants from Eastern Europe. Moreover, many economic opportunities were even open to the average man among the immigrants. The number of wealthy Jews in the western countries was increasing and their standard of living was rising. Consequently, a growing variety of jobs was now available for which the immigrants were well fit.[13] There were also great opportunities for rabbis, scholars, teachers, and authors. Wealthy Jews were eager to support learned immigrants in many ways. Jacob Emden says that in 1720 "Germany was at the peak of her success and wealth," referring of course, to Germany's Jewish society. He says further that he was advised to go to Metz and Mannheim where he would find it easy to sell many copies of his father's *Responsa*. His friends assured him that there he would receive "full handfuls of goodness" (*Shabbath* 62b).[14] Scholars in Poland were well aware of these opportunities. Rabbi Avi'ezri Selig Margalioth, author of *Hiburei Liqutim*, reports that "in our days, when scholars are confronted with hardships, they immediately leave the school and go to Germany to make money and amass wealth."[15] To be sure, he looked upon this with contempt. But ultimately he too went to Germany and became a resident scholar in the *Klaus* established in Halberstadt by the famous magnate Behrend Lehmann. With the situation in Poland as desperate as it was, a scholar could hardly withstand the temptation to emigrate when great opportunities beckoned to him in the West.

In general the attitude of the Jewish communities in western countries toward immigrants from Poland continued to be favorable. True, here and there we find a community that was unfriendly to immigrants and fought them. As early as 1714 the Jews of Berlin asked the government not to issue *Schutzbriefe* to new arrivals and even threatened to excommunicate their co-religionists who managed to settle in the city illegally. On the whole, however, the feeling of Jewish solidarity prevailed and the communities and their leaders continued to extend helping hands to the immigrants from the East. In 1719 the Jewish community of Fürth secured the right to maintain a public dining hall for wandering Jews. This same community often failed to inform the government of the arrival of immigrants. The Jewish community of Landsberg in Prussia, an important point of entry from Poland, acted in like manner. When the duchy of Ansbach decided to bar the entrance of wandering Jews in 1739, the court-Jew Isaac Nathan succeeded in obtaining from the authorities the privilege of having some of them admitted on his personal recommendation.[16] This was a period when the Jewish communities in the Germanies also created a huge number of fictitious communal jobs to enable alien Jews to settle in their midst as "communal functionaries."

II

The attitudes of the western governments toward immigrants also lacked uniformity during the first half of the eighteenth century. In general, however, they were now less friendly. The reluctance to admit immigrants from Poland primarily affected *Betteljuden,* but the governments' unfriendly attitudes were also manifested in the case of "regular" immigrants who could be integrated into the economies of the various countries.

A striking example was the change in the attitude of the Prussian government that in preceding decades had been fairly friendly toward immigrants. As long as Frederick I was alive (till 1713), immigrants were treated with patience and compassion. True, he also wanted to make sure his country would not be filled with "superfluous Jewish folk." But his first rigid order against *Betteljuden,* issued in 1712, still clearly instructed officials to have compassion for those "who behave well" and not to expel them. When Frederick William I (1713-1740) ascended the throne, a more hostile policy was initiated. Occasionally he decreed various local expulsions. Several times attempts were made to stop immigration from Poland because of epidemics that raged there. In 1718 and again in 1722 the king made special efforts to stop the infiltration of Polish Jews into East Prussia. Truly sharp measures were taken against immigration in 1730. The government began to limit the number of Jewish families in the country by decreeing a *numerus certus* for Jews in cities and towns. Also, a tight control was imposed on Jewish marriages. This policy, however, did not remain consistent. In 1734 Jewish war refugees from Poland were admitted to the provinces of Neumark and Pomerania, as we have seen. Somewhat later, again a more rigid policy was initiated, this time with regard to the Jews in Berlin. In April 1737 the government decided that only 120 Jewish families should be permitted to live in the capital. An additional 250 Jews were allowed to stay as communal fuctionaries and servants. The Prussian government thus wished to limit the Jewish population of Berlin to about 750. Within two months, indeed, close to 400 Jews left the city. When Frederick the Great ascended the throne (1740), he continued his father's anti-Jewish policy in an even more severe form. To be sure, the anti-Jewish tendencies of the two kings were partly softened by officialdom, which was largely made up of men with progressive attitudes. When Frederick I attempted to stop the immigration of Polish Jews to East Prussia, local officials energetically demanded their continued admission. As a result of all this, the Prussian kings of the first half of the eighteenth century generally failed to limit the number of Jews in their country, but their policy did adversely influence immigration from Poland.[17] Had they continued the traditional friendly policy toward immigrants, many more Polish Jews would have settled in Prussia. Of those who did, many had to live in the country illegally. This can be seen in the taxpayer rolls of the Jewish community of Berlin. Almost all the Polish Jews in possession of *Schutz-briefe* had already been living there before 1730. The "Polish" taxpayers after the year 1730 were invariably either widows or sons of immigrants.[18] In conclusion it should also be stressed that all through the first half of the century the Prussian government pursued a lenient policy with regard to the admission of Jewish teachers.[19]

Silesia, another country bordering on Poland, now also manifested a sharper opposition to Jewish immigration. This policy was a result of the fact that the immigrant population had grown considerably. As early as the end of the seventeenth century the government became alarmed by the continuous rise of the Jewish population. It was well known in Silesia that the adverse conditions in neighboring Poland were forcing Jews to emigrate. The situation is characterized by the fact that when the Jews of Lublin were in danger of being expelled in 1737, the Silesian government feared they would enter its territory and therefore issued strong orders not to admit them. A year later an additional step was taken when Charles VI (1711-1740) ordered the expulsion of all poor Jews from the province. In Bohemia, too, the earlier attempts to limit the number of Jews in Prague were continued. From 1703 to 1715 efforts were made in this direction. With the expulsion of the Jews in 1745, Bohemia for the time being lost its place on the map of Jewish migrations. The attitude toward immigrants in Moravia had also become less friendly. The emperor introduced strict controls on the Jewish population in order to sharply limit its further increase.[20]

During most of this period Saxony continued to manifest hostility toward Jews, and in particular immigration. In 1708 the few Polish Jews who had succeeded in settling there were expelled, together with other alien Jews. Beginning in 1733, when Count Heinrich Brühl became the all powerful official, a favorable change took place in the state's Jewish policy. To be sure, various decrees against Jewish participation in economic life were later issued to appease the burgesses of Dresden and Leipzig. Yet, the general attitude toward the Jewish population and new immigrants was friendlier than before.[21]

The attitude toward immigration in various places in western and southern Germany had also become less hostile to a certain degree. In Mayence, where old restrictions against Jewish immigration were renewed in 1720, the authorities later began to make the laws more lenient. Special consideration was given to immigrants who were prospective communal functionaries. In Fürth the authorities considerably reduced the fee scholars were required to pay for the right of residence. However, in Kassel the employment of new teachers from Poland was prohibited. In the state of Baden, Mannheim alone manifested a friendly attitude toward Jews and Jewish immigrants.[22]

In northern Germany the Hanseatic city of Lübeck again admitted a small number of Jews. A new policy of major importance was initiated by Denmark in 1729. Jews were now to be allowed to enter Altona and three other cities in the provinces of Schleswig and Holstein without special permits. Neighboring Hamburg, however, was hostile to the immigrants, especially during the first decade of the century when epidemics were raging in Poland.[23]

We see that during this period no uniform policy was pursued by the German states in regard to immigration from

Poland. Moreover, the Jewish policies of the individual states were unstable and often changed from one extreme to another. Occasionally the various governments also granted to court-Jews or other economically important men the privilege of introducing additional Jewish families into their countries.[24] A more unified policy developed in the Germanies with regard to *Betteljuden,* as we shall see later.

III

During the first half of the eighteenth century emigrants also originated from all parts of the Polish commonwealth. This was known in Western Europe where official documents stated that immigrants were arriving from Poland and Lithuania, the two parts of the commonwealth.[25] Again, an overwhelming majority of the emigrants were inhabitants of the regions adjacent to the western borders of the country. In fact, the percentage of these emigrants was even larger than in the second half of the seventeenth century. The main Jewish communities of the region of Posen, Krotoschin, Lissa, and Kalisz, are again mentioned in most of the sources as former homes of emigrants.[26] Of the 13 proofreaders from Poland who worked in the Hebrew printing presses in Dessau, Halle, Jesnitz, and Cöthen, 10 were from border regions, while only 3 were from other parts of Poland. Moreover, of these 10 immigrants, 6 came from the vicinity of Posen, 3 from Cracow or vicinity, and one from Lithuania. The situation was similar in London. Among the immigrant proletariat we find Jews from Posen, Lissa, and Brest Litovsk.[27] This becomes even more evident when we analyze the places of origin of the Jews who lived in Berlin in that period. Of the 42 families that can positively be identified as immigrants from Poland, 36 came from western Poland and Cracow, while only 6 originated elsewhere in the commonwealth. Here, too, Jews from Krotoschin (12 families), Lissa (7), and Kalish (5) constituted a majority of the immigrants from

Poland. Olkusz, located northwest of Cracow close to the border of Silesia, also contributed a relatively large number of immigrants.[28]

This pattern is confirmed by our sample list of 160 emigrants collected from many sources. About 70 percent came from areas on the western borders: Lithuania and the regions of Posen and Cracow. Only 30 percent came from other parts of the commonwealth (the area from Kielce to Lublin, present day East Galicia, and the Ukraine). The sample list also shows the vicinity of Posen with Krotoschin, Lissa, and Kalisz was the area that contributed the largest percentage of emigrants. The Ukraine, the easternmost province of the Polish commonwealth, contributed only 3 percent.

IV

Of all the western countries, the Germanies in this period absorbed most of the emigrants from Poland to an even larger degree than during the second half of the seventeenth century. In 1708 Rabbi Hirsch Auerbach of Brody wrote that "Germany had become a refuge for Jews from Poland." As we have seen, the author of *Hiburei Liqutim* also stated that whenever the living conditions of a scholar became unbearable, he immediately left for Germany. Prussia was once again the destination of at least half of all Polish Jewish immigrants to Germany. From an official document of 1708 we learn that the Prussian government did not know the exact number of Polish Jews living in the state.[29] About the same time a group of Polish Jews went to Neustettin to escape the troubles of the Great Northern War. The sources clearly show that many Polish Jews succeeded in settling in Prussia under various pretexts. A device used quite often was to pose as teachers who, as we recall, were admitted upon the recommendations of Jewish communal authorities.[30] Of major importance was the fact that early in the century Polish Jews managed to settle in Königsberg, the East Prussian capital, in spite of the opposition of the citizenry. At first the immigrants were admitted for a limited period of time. The permit was repeatedly renewed, however, and ultimately they became permanent inhabitants of the city. Some of them settled in neighboring villages. We have seen that the attempts occasionally made by the king to stem Jewish immigration into East Prussia were unsuccessful. By the 1740s a second generation of Polish Jews had grown up in Königsberg and signs of an economic rise became visible among them. At the same time Polish Jews settled in some ten small towns close to the Polish border, including Lyck and Johannisburg, which became very famous as centers of Hebrew printing in the nineteenth century. Other Polish Jews settled on the estates and in the courts of the East Prussian nobility.[31]

The Polish Jewish population in the capital city of Berlin also grew. It had already been of some significance at the close of the seventeenth century. The sources of the first half of the eighteenth century list many new names of Polish Jews. Most of them arrived in the first decades of the century and had succeeded in obtaining *Schutzbriefe*. There were also "illegal" Polish Jews in the city.[32] New immigrants from Poland had then appeared in other localities of the Prussian state, too, such as Frankfort on the Oder, Halberstadt and vicinity, Halle, Friedland, and in the province of Brandenburg. A settlement of Polish Jews also grew up in Landsberg, where the citizenry found that in a town so close to the border it was impossible to prevent the establishment of a large community of Jewish immigrants. The case of the town of Treuenbrietzen is interesting. In 1723 its 25 Jews were all immigrants from Poland, and they continued to arrive. The only exceptions were the Prussian territories in western Germany that at this time, it seems, absorbed few Jews from Poland, if any. The native Jewish population in these provinces was far from wealthy and opportunities to earn a livelihood were rather limited.[33] The sample list of immigrants mentioned above also shows that about half of those who settled in the Germanies made their homes in Prussia.

Polish Jewish emigrants were again going to Saxony after the expulsion of 1708. Their number, however, was rather small. Immigrants from Poland became somewhat more numerous after 1733 when, as we have seen, Count Brühl initiated his friendlier policy toward them.[34]

In northern Germany, Hamburg continued to be a major point of attraction to immigrants from Poland, in spite of the hostility the government manifested during the first decade of the century. The sources contain information about Jews from all walks of life who arrived there during this period. In the area of Hildesheim we also find a certain number of families from Poland, and a similar situation prevailed in Hanover.[35] Our sample list indicates that about 10 percent of the emigrants found homes in northern Germany.

The sources show that immigrants from Poland settled in many cities in the western and southern parts of Germany, such as Kassel, Fulda, Friedberg, Hanau, Frankfort on the Main, Offenbach, Düsseldorf, Worms, Mannheim, Karlsruhe, Mergentheim, and Heilbronn. We also again find immigrants in various small towns in these regions. An important destination seems to have been Offenbach, where we find Jews from areas in Poland such as Cracow, Brest Litovsk, and Zamosc. It should be safe to assume that Jews from Poland found refuge in Fürth during this period too. The reduction in the amount paid by scholars for the right of residence, as mentioned above, probably attracted a number of them.[36] The data contained in our sample list of emigrants show that 10 percent settled in western and southern Germany.

A large stream of Polish Jews made Altona their destination. This was the case especially after 1729 when the Danish government made it possible for Jews to settle there without special permits. At the same time we find new immigrants from Poland in Moisling, which was also under Danish control. All through the eighteenth century Polish Jews arrived in increasing numbers in the capital city of Copenhagen too.[37]

A review of Polish Jewish immigration into the lands of

the Hapsburg monarchy in this period reveals there was a definite decline in the number of migrants to Moravia. We no longer find large groups of immigrants in the various cities and towns, although there were individuals or small groups of Jews from Poland in about a dozen localities. Among the places that attracted them were important cities, such as Brünn, Nikolsburg, Kremsier, Eibenschütz, Ranitz, and Boskowitz.[38]

At this time some Polish Jews again settled in Vienna. The Jewish community there became quite small after the expulsion of 1670, but a limited number of Polish immigrants, most of whom were scholars and communal functionaries, found refuge under the protection of the wealthy Jewish families the imperial government permitted to live in the capital.[39]

Polish Jewish immigration continued to flow into Silesia, despite the opposition of the provincial government. It is safe to assume the complaint of the government that illegal Jewish immigrants from Poland were uninterruptedly streaming into the country was not without foundation. But it is hard to determine whether this immigration was of wide scope.[40] True, the sources provide us with information about individuals from Poland who settled in Glogau and Breslau. But all in all, information is rather scarce. It is also noteworthy that our sample list has only a few names of immigrants living in Silesia.[41]

Polish Jews also continued to migrate to Holland, both by land and by sea, although on a rather small scale. An emigrant from Zagory in Lithuania, who eventually reached Surinam, had sailed from Libau to Holland. A rabbi, who went there to have his book printed, wrote, "I traveled on the seas and my destination was the community of Amsterdam." In various sources we find information about individuals who emigrated to Holland, especially to the three large cities, Amsterdam, Rotterdam, and The Hague.[42]

Apparently, a somewhat stronger stream of Polish emigrants went to France at the turn of the century. We have seen that the 1701 edition of the dictionary *Safah Verurah* included a French translation of its entire vocabulary. The editor indicated on the title page that the dictionary would be of help to those "who go to other countries." To be sure, we should assume this edition reflects migratory movements prior to 1700, but we may assume a similar situation prevailed for at least some time after that year. Rabbi Jonathan Eibenschütz relates that in the years of his residence in Metz (1741-1750), yeshivah students from Poland came to the city. We also find here and there Polish rabbis who went as far as southern France to occupy positions in various communities.[43] Names of individuals who migrated from Poland to France are mentioned in the sources rather infrequently.

England, too, was a destination for Jewish emigrants from Poland during this period. In a membership list of London's Great Synagogue covering the years 1708-1750, at least six families can positively be identified as immigrants from Poland. Various other sources also mention Polish Jews who went to England and Ireland at this time.[44] Our sample list has a rather small number of names of emigrants to England. In conclusion it should be noted that a few Polish Jews also settled in the colonies in North America.[45]

During this period we encounter more families than before who did not immediately settle in new homes permanently after their departure from Poland, but lived successively in various countries in the West. An emigrant author mentioned above tells us explicitly that he "passed through several countries." There were families that first immigrated to Germany and then to England. For example, Moses Isaac of Meseritsch, who first lived in Frankfort (on the Main?), went to England in 1748. Isaac Pollack, reader in the Great Synagogue in London, came from Hamburg. The sons of a Polish Jewish family that had settled in Silesia before 1700 went from there to England, and later some of them sailed to North America. The children of an emigrant from Brest Litovsk, who arrived in England early in the century, also went to America. Rabbi Judah Löb of Krotoschin is a good example of an individual who lived in various countries in the West. He first immigrated to Austria, then to Germany and Holland, and ultimately to Carpentras in southern France, where he settled as rabbi of the community.[46] Another example is Rabbi Samuel Helman, also of Krotoschin. He first went to Prague to study in its yeshivah, and later held rabbinic positions in Moravia, Germany, and France. The cases described above suggest that a tendency to go farther west now began to develop among the emigrants from Poland. We will see later that this tendency was considerably intensified in the second half of the century.

V

Although the bulk of emigrants was largely composed of families, the number of single men was proportionately greater than in the preceding period. This is illustrated by the following examples. Five Jews from Poland living in Hildesheim or vicinity in 1732 were all married to native Jewish women, indicating, of course, that they went to Germany as young unmarried men.[47] In Plymouth we find an immigrant from Poland who arrived in England at the age of twenty.

An analysis of the occupations of emigrants reveals that scholars and merchants again composed the two largest groups. The proportion of scholars was even greater than in the second half of the preceding century. Jacob Emden complained that Polish scholars were occupying most of the rabbinic positions in the West, and Christian missionaries were aware of the fact that Poland was the country *woher man alle Rabbinen hole* (whence all rabbis are brought). These observations are supported by a wealth of information in the sources about scholars from Poland who held rabbinic positions in the West.[48] About half of the 200 emigrants in a sample list (compiled from various sources) were rabbis or other religious functionaries. Teachers from Poland were also a familiar sight in the West. A contemporary author wrote that "everybody [in Poland] desires to become a teacher in . . . Germany." The descriptions of Jewish life in Emden's memoirs show, indeed, that the Germanies of his time were swarming with *melamdim* from Poland. Their domination of the educational field is exemplified by the fact that in 1722 four Polish teachers were employed by the rather small community of Kassel. A better example is the fact that 17 of the 18 teachers employed by the Jews of Bützow from 1738 to 1769 were from Poland. This situation was made possible by the readiness of the governments to admit teachers from Poland, as we have seen above.[49]

In addition to rabbis and *melamdim*, a large number of nonprofessional scholars also went west to seek financial support from wealthy philanthropists. Likewise, Polish yeshivah students went to the Germanies to enter *Klausen* established by rich men. Older scholars and authors, too, continued to be numerous among the residents of the *Klausen*. Philanthropists frequently supported the publication of rabbinic works by these scholars. A typical example is the case of Azriel ben Moses Meshel of Vilna who went to Germany with his sons "to study, teach, and earn a livelihood, using their knowledge." Rabbi Margalioth, an emigrant cited above, describes the sharp competition among learned immigrants to gain the support of philanthropists. The struggles of the scholars vividly resemble the similarly motivated quarrels among Jewish humanists in Italy during the Renaissance.[50]

The percentage of merchants among the emigrants of this period was also large, especially in the Germanies. In the 1730s we find wealthy Jewish refugees from Poland in the Prussian provinces of Pomerania and Neumark. In a list of nearly 300 Jewish householders living in Berlin in 1749, the overwhelming majority were either businessmen or bankers. Since immigrants from Poland constituted about 10 percent of the taxpayers of the Jewish community, it is safe to assume that most of the Polish Jews belonged to the merchant class.

The sources indicate the occupations of a number of them. For example, in 1733 Joseph of Chmielnik owned a haberdashery; in 1749 a certain Joseph Pollack was a dealer in silk materials; and Aaron of Lissa earned his livelihood as a publisher and bookseller. Immigrants who settled in the border town of Landsberg traded in hides imported from Poland. In Karlsruhe we find an immigrant who dealt in precious stones. During this period, too, at least twenty visitors to the Leipzig fairs from localities in the Germanies were Polish immigrants. To be sure, we also find in various places numerous immigrants selling old clothes. The immigrant settlement in Königsberg had a diversified character which resembled the economic structure of Polish Jewry of that time. Its members were artisans, shopkeepers, innkeepers, and brokers. In ten small towns in East Prussia, Polish Jews earned their livelihood as innkeepers.[51] This occupation was widespread among Jews in the Polish commonwealth.

The number of Polish Jewish merchants who settled in Holland in this period was apparently much smaller. Our sample list shows that the emigrants to Holland were mainly rabbis and other religious functionaries. Literary and documentary sources also have little to say about merchants who immigrated to the Netherlands. Holland had already lost much of its significance as a world center of trade and the economic decline was quite noticeable among Dutch Jews. Consequently, the more enterprising individuals among emigrants chose the Germanies as their future home rather than more distant Holland. The few Polish Jews to be found in the Americas at this time were mostly merchants or plantation owners. The high cost of passage and the capitalistic nature of the American economy obviously favored the immigration of the more wealthy.[52]

The sources also occasionally report about various types of artisans and employees among the emigrants, such as a cook, a barber, and a brewer. Ample information is available about printers and proofreaders who chiefly immigrated to Prussia.[53] Our sample list shows that craftsmen and various types of employees constituted about 10 percent of the emigrants.

VI

In this period wandering Jews were a much larger segment of the emigration than in preceding times. Official documents confirm that again they came from Poland and Bohemia.[54] As early as 1707 there was rarely a day when less than thirty or forty wandering Jews stayed at the Jewish communal hostel in Ansbach. They usually arrived with their wives and children, and like true emigrants, brought from the old home whatever possessions they had. Rabbi Jonathan Eibenschütz described in biblical verses the ordeal endured by wandering yeshivah students who went from Poland to Metz. They trudged "almost two hundred miles . . . their shoes were worn and their feet swollen . . . and they wandered without strength . . . like starving gazelles." We may assume this description fitted all the wandering Jews in this period.

The increased immigration of poverty stricken Jews immediately evoked sharp opposition from the western governments. As early as 1712 the Prussian government issued a stern warning to all inhabitants of border regions not to extend any help to incoming wanderers. Those immigrants who had already crossed the border were to be given alms and sent back to Poland. The order threatened that any wanderer attempting to reenter Prussia would be heavily punished but evidently failed to achieve its objective. Between 1719 and 1750 the Prussian government found it necessary to issue more orders against *Betteljuden.* The law of 1750 attempted to involve Jewish communal authorities in the effort to stop the infiltration of wanderers.

Hanover again surpassed all other states in cruelty toward wandering Jews. An order issued in 1702 resembled earlier ordinances in general. However, the law of 1710 introduced new types of punishment to be inflicted upon unwanted immigrants. They were to be flogged and then sentenced to forced labor. Their children were to be taken away from them and placed in orphanages. Four years later a new order established another system of penalties. Upon his first attempt to enter the territory, a wanderer was to be deported, on his second attempt he was to be branded, and on his third attempt he was to be hanged. It appears that even the threats of mutilation and execution did not succeed in keeping wandering Jews away. New laws were issued against them at frequent intervals. In the 1720s and 1730s, however, the state of Hanover somewhat relaxed its opposition to *Betteljuden*. Orders against them were issued less frequently and wandering Jews "of good repute" were permitted to remain for short periods.[55]

Other states in the Germanies, too, each in its own way, fought the immigration of wandering Jews. In Fürth, for example, laws were issued against *Betteljuden* in 1713 and 1714. In the bishopric of Strassburg orders to expel all wandering Jews were issued in 1730 and 1732. The duke of Ostfriesland allowed their admission into his territory only with the approval of his court-Jew. A wanderer entering without such recommendation was to be flogged.[56]

The above examples show that *Betteljuden* had spread all over the Germanies during this period and that the governments tried to bar their entrance in various ways. In 1736 one prince submitted a plan to the German states for unified action against the wanderers. He suggested the *Betteljuden* problem should be put on the agenda of the all-German diet. The available information shows the matter was discussed among representatives of several governments, but we do not know whether it was actually taken up by the diet. The only known result was some states that had previously tolerated wandering Jews began to persecute them.[57] The fact that steps were taken to put the problem of wandering Jews before the *Reichstag* demonstrates how serious it had become.

Although the western governments usually called wandering Jews *Betteljuden* (beggar Jews), it was well known that not all of them belonged to this category. True, many were beggars and some even joined the underworld, but these constituted only a part of the mass of wandering Jews. Some were scholars or rabbis. The Prussian law of 1750 explicitly stated that *gelehrte Juden* (scholars) should be admitted upon the recommendation of Jewish communal authorities. The class of itinerant merchants was even larger. The conditions prevalent in Western Europe continued to be favorable to ambulant traders. Many of the laws against wanderers reveal there was a fear of competition from itinerant peddlers. Both the Prussian law of 1712 and the "Constitution" granted to the Jewish community of Fürth in 1719 rigidly prohibited the ambulant trade of wandering Jews. These two laws explicitly referred to new immigrants; Fürth's used the term *Betteljuden*. In 1720 the municipal authorities of Landsberg demanded that wandering Jews from Poland be denied permission to trade. A decade later the regional administration of the duchy of Geldern asked the central government in Berlin for copies of the laws against Jewish peddlers. The officials wanted to use these laws against alien Jews who were coming into the duchy with their merchandise. All this clearly shows that a sizable portion of the wandering Jews were not beggars but rather *Packenträger* (ambulant merchants).[58]

The Jewish communities in the Germanies found themselves in a difficult position in regard to *Betteljuden.* The governments used various pressures to force them to become partners in the fight against wanderers. But feelings of compassion toward their unfortunate and homeless brethren induced the communities to extend them a helping hand. Some communities, such as Berlin and Frankfort on the Main, did collaborate with the authorities in the effort to keep wandering Jews away. We have seen how in 1714 the Jewish communal authorities of Berlin were willing to use the threat of excommunication to expel illegal Jews. A satirical poem published in 1708 describes the cruelty of an official of the Jewish community of Frankfort on the Main to wandering Jews.

In most cases, however, the communities and influential individuals gave substantial aid to wanderers. A document of 1735 stated that *Schutzjuden* (legal Jewish residents) in Saxony were giving lodging to alien Jews, including beggars. To make this possible they used all kinds of pretexts, especially the one that they were employing the wanderers as servants. In some territories, such as Ansbach and Ostfriesland, court-Jews had the right to admit wandering Jews.

It is obvious that all these measures only benefited a small number of *Betteljuden*. The masses were forced to remain perpetual wanderers. To meet this situation the communities systematically began to build hostels suitable for housing large numbers of transients. Events that took place in the district of Mittelfranken illustrate the situation in Bavaria. In 1719 the region was flooded with about 800 wandering Jews from Poland and Bohemia. In spite of the hostile attitude of the authorities, the Jewish communities of Öttingen and Harburg requested permission to build hostels for *Betteljuden*. In the same year the Jews of nearby Fürth were granted the right to maintain a public dining hall for wanderers. Similar institutions were established in other parts of the Germanies during this period. A Jewish communal hostel also existed in Landsberg which, as we have seen, was an important crossing point used by Polish Jews when they entered the Brandenburg-Prussian territories.[59]

VII

There seems to be no way of determining the exact number of Jews who left their homes in Poland to emigrate to the West during this period. However, the sources again help us to obtain a general picture of the size of the migratory movement. Jacob Emden's memoirs are full of reports concerning Polish immigrants and their activities. An itinerant German missionary recalled that on his journeys he used to meet "Polish Jews." One gets the impression that their influx into

Germany was a continuous process. True, it appears that in this period more emigrants left Poland without their families than in the preceding one. However, the available information concerning individual emigrants shows that most of them did emigrate with their families. We also notice that each family consisted of at least five or six persons.[60] These observations lead us to conclude that the number of immigrants from Poland who settled in the Germanies was quite large. If the estimate that between 1700 and 1750 the Jewish population in Germany grew from some 25,000 to around 65,000 is correct, it should be safe to assume that this was largely due to the influx of immigrants from Poland.[61] Moreover, if we consider that during this period many Jews in the Germanies were converted to Christianity and that many states imposed limitations on Jewish marriages, we may perhaps assume that most of the increase of the Jewish population in the Germanies was due to the immigration of Polish Jews.

The sources leave no doubt that many of the immigrants who entered Prussia came with their families. The situation in the town of Treuenbrietzen, whose four Jewish families and the *melamed* they employed were all from Poland, may well be characteristic of other towns.[62] Additional information is available regarding other cities. In Neustettin, for example, there were 12 Polish Jewish families between 1713 and 1717. In Königsberg the Jews from Poland constituted at least half the Jewish population throughout the first half of the eighteenth century. If we give credence to statements made by the local citizenry, we may assume that at least 30 Jewish families from Poland and Lithuania were living in Königsberg as early as 1703. A trustworthy source indicates that at least 45 Polish Jewish families were living there in 1751. It seems that as time went on the proportion of Polish immigrants in that community declined because of the influx of German Jews. The total number of Polish Jews living in the previously mentioned border towns in East Prussia must have been considerable. Most likely the immigrant

71

population in the border town of Landsberg was also large but its exact size is unknown. More accurate information is available about Berlin. In 1734 the government brought to the attention of the Jewish community the fact that there were "many Polish Jews" in the city. An analysis of the lists of taxpayers of the Jewish community reveals that about 10 percent were Polish immigrants. Since in all likelihood there was a large number of Polish Jews among the poor, nonpaying members of the community, we may infer Polish immigrants constituted at least 15 percent of Berlin's total Jewish population. The number of immigrants was probably between 250 and 300. It may also be assumed that some of the 400 Jews banished from the city in 1737 were poor immigrants from Poland. However, almost all the taxpaying immigrants and their families remained in Berlin after this partial expulsion.[63]

Accurate figures are not available for northern Germany either, but we have ample information about immigrants who settled with their families in cities like Hamburg, Altona, and Hanover. After 1729 the immigrant population in Altona rose because many took advantage of the permission of free settlement. The situation in Moisling was similar. An impressive number of Polish scholars resided in the *Klausen* of Hamburg and Altona. The above facts imply, of course, that northern Germany's immigrant population was quite large. There were at least 5 Polish immigrant families among the 80 Jewish families living in the Hildesheim region in 1732, thus constituting about 6 percent of the Jewish population.[64] As to western Germany and Bavaria, it can only be said that its Polish immigrant population consisted mostly of families rather than individuals. (Members of at least one family represented three generations.) There seems to be no way, however, of obtaining any precise figures. Similarly, very little can be said about the size of the immigrant population in the Hapsburg territories. It should be stressed, however, that the information we do have concerning the emigrants who went to Moravia, also pertains to families rather than individuals.[65]

Likewise, we cannot estimate the number of Polish immigrants who settled in England during this period. There
are indications that their number was of some significance,
although it was not very large. Polish Jewish immigration to
Holland at this time was also rather limited, as we have
seen. The available figures concerning the growth of Amsterdam's Jewish population between 1674 and 1748 confirm this.
In the forty-six years from 1674 to 1720, the city's Ashkenazic
population grew from 5,000 to 9,000, an increase of 80 percent
or about 100 persons a year. In the almost thirty years between 1720 and 1748, however, the Ashkenazic population
increased by but 1,000. This was only a 10 percent gain,
with an average rate of 35 persons a year.[66] This analysis
clearly shows that only a few alien Jews immigrated to Amsterdam during most of the first half of the eighteenth century. It may safely be assumed the situation in other Dutch
cities was similar.

We have seen that the immigration of Polish Jews to
France during this period was probably somewhat larger,
although there seems to be no way of determining the exact
number. That the number of Polish Jews who settled in America at this time was small was pointed out above.

The above observations regarding the number of emigrants refer to "regular" newcomers—those able to settle permanently. There were many more *Betteljuden*, however, during this period. Governments continued to complain that
"many beggars" were coming from Poland and Bohemia. In
1750 reports stated that on each Jewish holiday large masses
of them converged upon Berlin. Although the loud complaints of the governments were probably exaggerated, the
fact is that wandering Jews were now arriving in much larger
numbers than during the seventeenth century. Had not their
numbers been growing alarmingly, the Hanoverian government would not have threatened them with branding and
hanging. This is further confirmed by the information that
as early as 1707, from 30 to 40 wanderers were residing daily
at the Jewish communal hostel in Ansbach. In 1719 during

a period of only four months, some 700 or 800 *Betteljuden* passed through the town of Harburg in Mittelfranken; at least 500 of them came from Poland. This information concerning a single region in Bavaria reflects a situation in which many thousands of Jewish wayfarers from Poland were wandering all over Western Europe. Their presence in England is manifested by the appearance of Polish Jews among the Jewish proletariat in London.[67]

VIII

Information amply available in the sources reveals that during the first half of the eighteenth century the integration of immigrants proceeded more rapidly than in the preceding period. This integration can best be observed in rabbinic families about whom biographical data are available in books written by their members. Often the process of integration of the common people can also be reconstructed. Little is known about emigrants who returned from the West to Poland. The taxpayer lists of the Jewish community in Berlin clearly indicate that while in the 1730s and 1740s many of the Polish immigrants of this period had died, their descendants continued to live in the city.[68] The situation was similar in other cities, such as Königsberg in East Prussia, Offenbach in western Germany, Vienna, and London. Throughout this period a growing number of immigrants from Poland succeeded in obtaining *Schutzbriefe* from German governments and thus entered the ranks of the local Jewish "aristocracy."[69]

In this period, too, a state of tension at first existed between newcomers and native Jews. The memoirs of Jacob Emden offer much information on this aspect of immigration. He reports that he was advised not to marry a woman from Poland because "their nature differs and does not harmonize with that of the people of these countries." Emden also considered the Polish Jews to be rather haughty.[70] Other

German Jews obviously had a different opinion, as the sources contain many cases of intermarriage between them and immigrants. Marcus Abraham, a well known immigrant from Lissa, successively married two women of prominent families in Berlin. The daughters of Moses Katzenellenbogen, an immigrant who held rabbinic positions in Fürth and Schwabach, married native Jews. The family of immigrant Rabbi Gabriel Eskeles intermarried with the family of a famous rabbi magnate, Samson Wertheimer. Another immigrant was related by marriage to Gershon Politz, chief rabbi of Moravia. These are only a few of many examples. Marriages between native Jews and immigrants who were not members of rabbinic families were not rare. We know of such cases in Berlin and Vienna, and other cities.[71]

The incidence of intermarriage between native Jews and immigrants suggests some of the latter achieved economic success rapidly. It is worth repeating that even *melamdim* were able "to make a fortune" in the Germanies. The taxpayer lists of Berlin clearly show that a sizable number of Polish immigrants enjoyed economic prosperity. In this period, too, at least twenty immigrants frequented the Leipzig fairs. The following data about individuals confirm the general picture. One of the first Polish Jewish settlers in Königsberg was able to open a new factory in 1724. Twelve years later his son built a factory in Tilsit and thus opened the city to Jewish settlement. It seems, however, that the Polish Jewish immigrants who arrived in England during the first half of the eighteenth century did not attain much economic success. A list of about 350 Jews who held Bank of England stock between 1694 and 1725 does not contain any names indicating Eastern European origin. However, at the same time an Eastern European Jew attained remarkable economic success in America. A young man who emigrated from Zagory in Lithuania and became a plantation owner in Surinam left such a large estate that his brothers' descendants received income from it down to our own times.[72] This same emigrant, incidentally, after arriving in Holland on his way to America, changed his name from Naphtali Cohen to Gerrit Jacobs. The acceptance of new names, such as Philip and Maria, by Polish emigrants became more common and was a further step in the process of acculturation.[73]

In this period the newcomers were much more active in Jewish communal affairs than before. To begin with, among them were many philanthropists whose charitable endeavors were quite impressive. One, Solomon of Meseritsch, was famous in Hamburg for the support he gave to needy scholars and the poor in general. In 1758 David ben Judah Löb, an immigrant to Fürth from Cracow, willed the large sum of 500 florins to the poor of the community. A man named Pollack was one of the founders of Amsterdam's Megadle Jethomim, a society for the care of orphans. Later, the name Pollack occurred quite often in the society's membership rolls. In 1741 Simon Pollack willed the huge sum of 10,000 florins to needy scholars. Polish Jews were active as *gabaim* (officers) of such communal institutions as societies for providing financial aid to the poor of the Holy Land, burial brotherhoods, and school committees.[74]

In a number of cities Polish immigrants were elected as *parnasim*, leaders of the Jewish communities. It is not surprising that an immigrant was head of the community of Königsberg, which had been founded by Polish Jews, but it is remarkable that immigrants served in similar positions in many other communities. They were often among the signatories of contracts given by communities to newly elected rabbis *(kithvei rabanuth)*. In London a Polish immigrant was appointed scribe of the community of 1738, and two of his sons succeeded him in this position. Thus father and sons were in the service of London's Jewish community for forty years. The importance achieved in the area of communal affairs by the previously mentioned immigrant from Lissa, Marcus Abraham, was remarkable. Early in this period Polish immigrants in Hamburg played equally important roles in Jewish communal affairs. A number of communal leaders in Holland were also immigrants or sons of immigrants. The following case is characteristic of the role immigrants played in Jewish communal affairs. In 1710 Solomon Lifschütz, a scholar from Lissa, was appointed rabbi of Rotterdam, after having held the same position in The Hague. His son Judah inherited the position after his death in 1736. When Judah died in 1754 and his son Abraham became a candidate for the post, opposition developed against him. The *parnasim* were close relatives of the candidate and there was concern the family might gain full control of the community. These examples, however, should not mislead us into believing that everywhere the integration of immigrants was complete. An analysis of the minutes book of Berlin's Jewish community reveals that invariably there were Polish immigrants among the second-ranking office holders in the community, such as the *gabaim* of various societies. Occasionally an immigrant also served on the election committee of the community (*kesherim*). But very rarely could an immigrant be found among the *parnasim*, the highest officers of the community.[75]

The influence of immigrants from Poland was most conspicuous in the area of the religious life of western Jewry. It is doubtful whether Jewish educational activities would have been possible without the large numbers of Polish *melamdim*. Their influence was of a much wider scope than was warranted by their position as teachers. According to Jacob Emden, the *melamdim* paved the way for Polish scholars to obtain so many leading rabbinic posts in the West. The bitter competition among *melamdim* is understandable only when we consider the influence they were able to exert on the Jewish aristocracy and communal leadership.

The influence of immigrant rabbis was even greater than that of the *melamdim*. It seems that Emden's dislike of Polish rabbis was not shared by his contemporaries. A good example is Rabbi Marcus Abraham of Lissa who was greatly respected in Berlin and elected head of the rabbinic court in 1726. Some immigrant rabbis established rabbinic "dynasties" in the Germanies, Holland, and England, which had a great influence upon the religious life of western Jewry. A few examples are presented here. Hirsch Harif, a *rosh-yeshivah* (head of a rabbinical school) in Lemberg, was elected rabbi of Halberstadt in 1718. The community agreed to support his yeshivah and a group of his students followed him to Halberstadt. Rabbi Hirsch was a respected leader of his community for thirty years until his death in 1748. Three of his five sons became rabbis in various communities in the Germanies. Moses Katzenellenbogen of Podhajce became head of a yeshivah in Fürth in 1700 and later was rabbi of Schwabach. His sons also were rabbis in the West, two in Germany (Wallerstein and Mannheim), the third in Alsace (Hagenau). A large rabbinic dynasty was founded by Baruch Kahana, who left Poland in 1710 to become rabbi of Fürth. The sources contain many cases of descendants of immigrant rabbis of this period holding rabbinic positions in the West inherited from their fathers. A good example is the rabbinic dynasty founded by Levi Saul Löwenstamm, who became Ashkenazic rabbi of Amsterdam in 1740. His position was inherited by his son Saul and later by his grandson Jacob Moses. During the second half of the eighteenth century, and throughout most of the nineteenth, their descendants held rabbinic positions in the most important communities of the West (London, Mannheim, Halberstadt, Berlin, Frankfort on the Oder, Breslau, Amsterdam, The Hague, and Rotterdam). Jonathan Eibenschütz, one of the greatest and most controversial rabbis of the eighteenth century, was also a native of Poland. His father left the country early in the century to become rabbi of Eibenschütz in Moravia. Jonathan, who as a boy went to Moravia with his father, later held rabbinic positions in important western communities. J. P. Callenberg, a famous Christian missionary, offered a striking testimony about the great religious role played by Polish rabbis in the West. He candidly admitted that during the period of widespread Christian conversion in the Germanies, the immigrant rabbis succeeded in stopping the trend and thus gave the Jews the strength to remain faithful to the God of their fathers.[76]

CHAPTER FOUR

The Second Half of the
Eighteenth Century

I

THE second half of the eighteenth century, like the first half, was a period of intensive migratory movement among the Jews of the Polish commonwealth. During this period new categories of emigrants appeared who went west for reasons different from those of earlier times. The movement of Polish emigrants to Holland and England that had not been strong in the first half of the century now again gained momentum. This also was a period when the movement of wandering Jews reached its peak and their never ending journies extended to the farthest regions of the West. The situation of the Polish commonwealth grew progressively worse under its last king, Stanislaw Augustus Poniatowski, who ruled from 1764 to 1795. Friction between the various social strata and ethnic groups was increasing. In the first partition of Poland (1772) the commonwealth lost a considerable amount of territory. A demoralizing anarchy was spreading throughout the country, which ultimately vanished from the map of sovereign states (1795). The situation of the Jews was also deteriorating. The burden of taxation became heavier and in addition various areas of the economy were closed to them. The never ending Cossack riots once again reached a point of explosion in 1768. The massacre of the Jews of Uman strongly resembled the cruel events of 1648-1649.[1]

The unbearable situation of the Jews during this period is amply reflected in the writings of emigrant authors. The rabbi of Stanisławów attempted to emigrate because of oppression by a local high official. A Lithuanian rabbi left his home to settle in England because of local unrest and economic stress. Joshua Shapiro, rabbi of Bialystok, emigrated to Schwerin in Mecklenburg "because of many adversities, troubles, and vexations." The evil actions of informers also continued to force rabbis from their homes. A group of rabbis from Lissa, for example, were among the victims of informers. One of Poland's greatest rabbis, Phineas Horowitz, whose life had been in danger twice, came to the conclusion that all social order was about to collapse as a result of the unceasing wars and insurrections. He therefore considered it his good fortune when he was offered the important position of rabbi of Frankfort on the Main in 1772. The Jewish communities in the Western World were aware of the connection between the tragic situation in Poland and the enlarged emigration from that country. In a communication to the government the Ashkenazic community of London, for example, maintained the situation in Poland was responsible for the arrival of large numbers of poor Jews in the city toward the end of the century.

In this period the desire for political freedom spreading among the Jews of Poland was another cause for emigration. This is attested by the peregrinations of the artist Solomon Bennett. After leaving his home town of Polotzk, he went to Copenhagen, and then to Berlin. There he realized the freedoms enjoyed by the Jews of Prussia were limited and he went to England, where he made his permanent home.[2] During this period emigrants again quite frequently stated that economic stress forced them to leave their homes. The famous grammarian Judah Löb Bensew, for example, went abroad to seek a livelihood. There were also many ordinary men who fled because of inability to pay their debts.[3]

In this period there emerged a new category of emigrants who decided to leave their homes for religious and cultural reasons. We have seen that during the first half of the century yeshivah students went from Poland to Metz and Frankfort on the Main. This practice also took place during the second half of the century. When Hirsch Janow was appointed rabbi of Fürth in 1778, most of his students followed him from Posen to Germany. In addition, men who had acquired secular knowledge were now attracted by the circles of the *haskalah* (Jewish Enlightenment movement) in the West. Isaac Euchel relates that Israel Samosch, one of Poland's early *maskilim* (adherents of the *haskalah*), left for Germany in 1740 because local fanatics persecuted him for his love of philosophy. Samosch himself also alluded to this in his writings. Emigrant *maskilim* appeared much more frequently after 1750. Persecution, however, was not the only cause for their migration. The new community of learning in Berlin centering around Moses Mendelssohn strongly attracted them. Solomon Maimon and Solomon Bennett represent this type of emigrant. Bennett, an innkeeper in Polotsk, had such a great desire to study the art of painting that he left his wife and children and went to Copenhagen. It is interesting to note that his wife and parents encouraged him to go on this *tour d'études*. In the 1760s Sabbathians and Frankists also began to leave Poland in groups. About the same time, while Jacob Frank was detained in Czestochowa, a certain Isaac Aaron Teomim went to Germany as a messenger of the Sabbathians. He met with other adherents of the dead messiah there and attempted to enlist the assistance of Christian scholars in obtaining permits for Polish Sabbathians to settle in Germany.[4]

In addition to the specific factors driving groups of people to emigrate, there was a general trend to leave the country. Aryeh Leibush Horovitz, rabbi in Stanislawów, implored his uncle Jacob Moses Löwenstamm, rabbi of Amsterdam, to make it possible for him to immigrate to Holland. He informed his uncle of his determination to seek refuge abroad. "O let me escape thither" (Genesis 19: 20). Men devoted to their families, such as Solomon Bennett and Raphael Cohn (later rabbi of the Ashkenazic community of Hamburg), were willing to leave their wives and children in Poland temporarily and go abroad in search of new homes. The urge to leave Poland is also evident in the case of Samuel, the young physician of the Jewish community of Inowrazlaw, whose "desire was strong to obtain a post in one of the cities in Germany." The philosopher Solomon Maimon was forced to go to Germany by a combination of the factors enumerated above. He left Poland because he found his economic position deteriorating and also realized he would have no opportunity of acquiring secular knowledge there. He later returned to Posen for a short time and became so disgusted by the fanaticism of the people that he decided he could no longer live in Poland.[5]

Throughout this period the possibilities of earning a livelihood in the western countries were quite favorable. Saul Löwenstamm, rabbi of Dubno, was extremely glad when he was offered the position of Ashkenazic rabbi of Amsterdam in 1755. He recorded his thoughts—"be strong and have courage . . . this big city is open to you; here you will live in comfort." Ordinary people and the lower ranks of the professional intelligentsia also had many opportunities. The sources show that between 1750 and 1800 there was a great demand for teachers and ritual slaughterers in the West. In 1772 the principal of a Jewish school in Potsdam suggested to Frederick the Great that alien *melamdim* should be admitted into Prussia on condition they become permanent residents. Every summer during the annual fair in Frankfort on the Oder a sort of "labor exchange" functioned at which *melamdim* and ritual slaughterers were hired by various communities in the Germanies. Even though only a *melamed*, a clever individual had many opportunities to make money. In *Kethav Yosher* (Berlin 1794), an anonymous satirical dialogue ascribed to Saul Levin, a *melamed* from Poland employed in Germany states, "I am, thank God, a ritual slaughterer . . . and in addition a Torah scroll scribe, Torah reader, *shofar* blower, cantor, circumciser, male nurse, and grave digger." The memoirs of Moses Wasserzug, a Polish *melamed* in Germany, show that this was not merely fantasy on an author's part. Wasserzug relates that he earned money in the Germanies as a teacher, cantor, ritual slaughterer, and *kashruth* supervisor, and also lent money on interest. All these different opportunities enticed many Polish Jews, tired of the hard life in their homeland, to emigrate to the Germanies.[6]

II

During the second half of the eighteenth century the western countries again did not have consistent policies in dealing with Jewish immigration from Eastern Europe. On one hand, a somewhat more liberal attitude was developing. In some states the authorities were no longer satisfied with merely issuing orders of expulsion against wandering Jews, but also began searching for other solutions to the problem. On the other hand, however, there was apprehension that a more liberal attitude would attract larger masses of Polish Jews to the West. An analysis of the actions taken by the various governments shows the inconsistencies of their policies. To begin with, also during this period various states expelled Jews, especially poor Jews. In 1784, for example, the authorities of Alsace banished all Jews who did not have permanent domiciles or were too poor to pay taxes. When Frederick the Great annexed a part of northwestern Poland (West Prussia) in the first partition of the commonwealth, his dislike for the multitude of his new Jewish subjects was so great that he decided to expel them to the still independent part of Poland. His more liberal officials succeeded in dissuading him from carrying out a general expulsion and ultimately only about 7,000 of the poorest Jews were sent to Poland between 1773 and 1784. The king also forbade the Jews of West Prussia to settle in other parts of the kingdom. In 1770 the state of Hanover, which was perpetually hostile to wandering Jews, issued an order prohibiting the admission of Polish Jews even when they had valid passports. The government of Austria also now manifested more openly its opposition to Jewish immigration. In their newly acquired Polish province of Galicia, the Austrians treated poverty stricken Jews in much the same way the Prussians treated Jews in West Prussia. During 1781 and 1782 the Austrians expelled about 2,000 Jews into what was left of the Polish commonwealth.[7]

Signs of changing attitudes, however, were noticeable everywhere. Occasionally opinions were expressed explicitly favoring the admission of Jewish immigrants. A quite forceful plea for Jewish immigration was made by an anonymous author in a pamphlet entitled *Über Aufnahme und Concessionierung der fremden und einheimischen Juden* (Berlin 1802). Abbé Gregoire discussed the subject, using a totally new approach. He strongly advocated that Jews should have the right to emigrate to other countries in order "to improve their situation." The new attitude was even noticeable in the treatment the immigrants received in Prussia. Solomon Maimon relates that Jews who arrived in Berlin by mail coach were allowed to enter. The story of his own arrival also suggests that once an immigrant was inside the city he could find a way to remain. Influential Jews, one of whom was also from Poland, were able to help him obtain a permit to stay. A Prussian law issued in 1780 against wandering Jews explicitly directed that those who possessed fifty thalers could be admitted. The ordinance even went as far as allowing the admission of beggars in cases where *Schutzjuden* declared them *domestiques*. The Prussians also became somewhat friendlier toward Jewish artisans from Poland. A number of cooks and tailors were permitted to settle in Breslau to serve the many Polish Jewish visitors to the annual fairs. In his famous treatise, *Über die bürgerliche Verbesserung der Juden*, Christian Wilhelm Dohm suggested that Prussia admit Jewish artisans from Poland to teach Jewish children their various trades. He felt this would greatly contribute to the productivity of Prussia's Jews.[8] Jewish immigrants were also treated in a more liberal way in other German states. The bishop prince of Paderborn, for example, permitted Polish Jewish peddlers to trade in his territory. In 1771 the duke of Ansbach stated that his duchy would gain by the immigration of wealthy Jews. Polish Jews were aware that the attitude of the western countries in regard to their immigration was becoming more favorable. The changing attitude is demonstrated by the fact that a group of Sabbathians attempted to secure the right of settlement in the West *prior* to their departure from Poland.[9]

The wavering and often contradictory policies of the western states in regard to Jewish immigration resulted from a strong fear there would be an onrush of Polish Jews who were psychologically ready for emigration. This fear was noticeable particularly during the last decades of the century when the number of wandering Jews was rapidly increasing, as will be seen later. Thus opposition to Jewish immigrants, especially Polish Jews, began to appear even in places previously friendly toward them. In Paderborn, for example, Polish Jewish peddlers were no longer allowed the privilege of trading and special precautions were taken to prevent them from entering the territory. In 1790 the Prussian government began to carefully observe the size of the Jewish population in Breslau in order to prevent the immigration of alien Jews, *besonders aber aus Polen* (especially those from Poland). Curiously, the fear of an imminent onrush of masses of Jewish immigrants from Poland was most prevalent in liberal England, in revolutionary France, and in Holland during the period of the Batavian Republic. At the end of the century the Lord Mayor of London, angered by the influx of alien Jews, informed the leaders of the Jewish community that all new immigrants must leave the city or else be forcibly deported. French statesmen angrily complained that ever since the revolutionary parliament had granted equality to Jews, immigrants from Poland and Germany had been converging upon the country. Several years later, similar complaints were voiced in the Dutch parliament during a debate on the emancipation of the Jews.[10] Justified or not, the fear of Jewish mass emigration from Poland strongly influenced the attitude of the various governments toward Jewish immigration.[11]

III

During this period, again, most of the Jewish emigrants came from western regions of the commonwealth and Lithuania. This characteristic, however, was now somewhat less conspicuous than before. The sources clearly indicate that Jews from other regions of the commonwealth were emigrating to the West in larger numbers. It is also noteworthy that the emigrants came from many more localities than in former times. An analysis of the 36 Polish Jewish immigrant families who lived in the territory of Mecklenburg-Schwerin in 1769 shows that they came from 27 towns.[12] Over half of these towns were located in western Poland, and the others were in central regions of the commonwealth.

A list of 105 Polish Jews who died in Königsberg, East Prussia, between 1770 and 1810 presents a basically similar picture. We find that 53 came from nearby Lithuania, 46 from western Poland, and a few from elsewhere. Almost all the Polish Jews who settled in Berlin during this period came from western parts of the country. Paradoxically, Jews from western Poland had to emigrate eastward to Königsberg in order to reach the Western World. This phenomenon was probably a result of the establishment of the Pale of Settlement by the Prussian government for the Jews of its newly acquired Polish territories. It was probably easier for Jews of the pale to go eastward to Königsberg than westward to Berlin. As a rule, however, emigrants were again crossing the border closest to their homes. Solomon Maimon, a Lithuanian, went west by way of Königsberg. Similarly, Solomon Bennett, an inhabitant of Polotsk, went westward through the port city of Riga. Also, most of the Polish Jews who immigrated to America during this period came from western parts of the commonwealth. In addition to the western cities of Posen, Kalisz, Krotoschin, and Lissa, nearby Flatow (Zlotowo) now became a place from which emigrants went west. Other cities and towns in the vicinity of Posen were also sending more emigrants to the West than previously.

Farther east was Zamosc, another community that many emigrants left to go west. It was one of the first centers of the *haskalah* in Poland and thus knowledge about the Western World was easily accessible to its inhabitants. Numerous *maskilim* left the city for western centers of Jewish culture. Ordinary men, too, went west because of adverse economic conditions. A number of Jews emigrated after a great fire devastated part of the city in 1768.[13]

Various contemporary documents tell about Ukrainian Jews who emigrated during the last decades of the eighteenth century. There is no foundation in the sources, however, for the often repeated statement that masses of Ukrainian Jews emigrated to the West after the massacre of Uman in 1768. It seems that during this period Jewish emigration westward from Galicia began to decrease. After Galicia became part of the Hapsburg monarchy, many of its Jews preferred to go to Hungary instead.[14]

A list of emigrants containing over 100 names assembled by the author confirms the conclusions offered by the sources. About 60 percent came from regions adjacent to the western borders and the rest from other parts of the commonwealth. About 10 percent were from the Ukraine.

IV

On their way west emigrants made use of all available means of transportation. It seems that now more of them went by ship. Emigrants from Lithuania and White Russia usually sailed from Riga or Königsberg. Those from western Poland left from Danzig. The low cost of passage to England was one of the factors that caused the influx of poor Polish Jews into Britain. Information concerning routes and means of transportation was now more easily available. When Solomon Maimon arrived in Königsberg, local Jews advised him to take a boat to Stettin and from there to go to Frankfort on the Oder. He was assured that after staying in Frankfort he could more easily enter Berlin.[15]

Germany was again the country that most strongly attracted emigrants. In this period Polish Jews penetrated more of Germany than formerly. During the first years of the nineteenth century when the Jews in German states were ordered to acquire surnames, a number of them chose Pollack. This indicates, of course, that they were immigrants and not descendants of immigrants.[16] Now, as before, Polish Jews were to be seen throughout the Germanies. The historian Marcus Jost, the son of a Polish immigrant, relates that during his boyhood many alien scholars passed through his home town, Bernburg (Anhalt), most of whom came from Poland.[17]

Despite the hostile attitude manifested by Frederick the Great, Prussia was again a major destination for emigrants from Poland. The sources offer ample information about individuals who went to Berlin. The lists of Jews granted citizenship (*Judenbürgerbücher*) show some twenty who had been born in Poland and settled in Berlin during this period.[18] Lazarus Bendavid, born in Berlin in 1762, relates that three of his five teachers were Polish Jews. A certain lodging house in Berlin was known as the place "where Polish Jews used to stay." Many Jewish immigrants from Poland were also living in other Prussian cities, such as Frankfort on the Oder and Halberstadt, and in various smaller localities, like Königsberg in the Neumark, Landsberg on the Warthe, and Dernburg. The province of East Prussia and its capital, Königsberg, continued to attract many immigrants. The same holds true for Silesia, now part of Prussia. The ever growing community of Polish Jews in Breslau was now the largest Jewish group in the city. Newly arrived immigrants from Poland also lived in the two old communities of Glogau and Zülz, and in other towns, such as Militsch.[19] Our list of some 100 immigrants to Germany, culled from various sources, shows that about half settled in the territories of Prussia, including Silesia. Polish Jewish immigration to Saxony was rather small during this period.[20]

The movement of Jewish emigrants from Poland into northern Germany continued to be strong. They could again be found in Hamburg, Hanover, Emden (which became part of Prussia in 1744), Hildesheim, and other cities. In addition, there exists detailed information concerning the situation in the duchy of Mecklenburg-Schwerin, which indicates that Polish immigrants also quite often settled in small towns. There were 36 immigrant families scattered throughout 31 Jewish communities in the duchy. It is worth noting that they settled in all parts of the duchy of Mecklenburg in spite of the widespread belief that a *heirem* (ban) on future Jewish settlement in the territory was promulgated after the expulsion of 1492. It seems, however, that the immigrants had a vague feeling of guilt and in 1752 they requested the rabbinic authorities to annul the *heirem*. After 1750 the number of Polish Jews in the duchy became much larger.[21]

The Danish possessions in northern Germany also continued to be a major destination for Polish emigrants. Many communal functionaries in Moisling were from Poland. At the turn of the century a Polish immigrant was appointed rabbi of the community. Polish Jews also lived in the port city of Kiel, which came under Danish control in 1773. The number of Polish Jewish immigrants in Copenhagen also increased, and in addition, many wandering Jews passed through the city. Altona continued to attract immigrants. The sources show that during this period wandering Jews often said their "domicile" was either Altona or Amsterdam. This indicates, of course, that these two cities were among the most popular destinations on the map of the Polish Jewish migratory movement. Our list of emigrants shows that about 20 percent settled in the north. A few Polish Jews were also able to settle in Sweden.[22]

More Polish Jews were now going to western Germany. Many immigrants, especially scholars, settled in Frankfort on the Main. In nearby Offenbach there were now more Polish Jews than in the first half of the century. A large number of them, followers of the false messiah Jacob Frank, began to settle in the vicinity of Offenbach in 1786 when their leader established his residence there. Polish Jews could also be found in Paderborn, as seen above, as well as in Hanau and Düsseldorf. It would be correct to assume that some of the "alien" Jews who settled in the city of Essen in 1775 were from Poland. Although there is no definite proof concerning the arrival of Polish Jews in other towns of western Germany, such as Mayence and Bonn, it should be pointed out that a number of Jews in those towns assumed the surname Pollack in 1808. Considering the increased immigration of Polish Jews to this region during the second half of the eighteenth century, it may be safely assumed that these Pollacks, or at least some of them, came prior to 1800.[23]

Little definite information is available concerning the arrival of Polish Jews in southern Germany. However, Jews whose family names indicate Polish origin were living in various towns, such as Mannheim, Karlsruhe, and Weinheim, during the first decade of the nineteenth century.[24] It may again be assumed that some of them came before 1800. Somewhat more definite but still scarce information is available about migrants from Poland who went to various regions of what is now Bavaria. Rabbis from Poland, accompanied by their yeshivah students, settled in Fürth, as seen above. Scholars from Poland, as well as common men, were residing in Ansbach, in the Upper Palatinate (Oberpfalz), and in the vicinity of Würzburg.[25] Our list of immigrants who settled in southern Germany, including Bavaria, is rather small.

A number of Polish Jews also settled in various provinces of the Hapsburg monarchy in this period. There was again a decrease in the number of Polish Jews who went to Moravia. It seems that most of them were rabbis, such as Samuel Horovitz, "the Rebbe Reb Schmelka," who became chief rabbi of Moravia with residence in Nikolsburg. Polish rabbis could also be found in Kremsier, Ungarisch Brod, Znaim, and other towns. Some laymen immigrants were also scattered throughout Moravia.[26] It seems that only a few Polish Jews went to Bohemia and information about individual immigrants is rather scarce. Instead, there was an increased migration to Vienna, where Jews from various regions in Poland, but primarily Galicia, now lived. There were Galician Jews in Vienna before the partitions of Poland gave the region to the Hapsburg monarchy. The number of Polish Jews in Vienna increased considerably around 1800. To be sure, Galician Jews could not legally immigrate to Vienna. In practice, however, many means were available for them to enter the city and remain illegally. For the first time Polish Jews, with their long garments, were so numerous in Vienna that they became a subject for caricaturists.[27] Our list of names of emigrants shows that 7 or 8 percent settled in Moravia and Austria during this period.

As was the case about a century before, Holland again became a major destination for a large number of Polish Jewish emigrants. Ample information is available regarding emigrant families who went to Amsterdam and other cities and towns, such as The Hague, Haarlem, and Amersfoort.[28] As may be expected, however, most of them went to Amsterdam. Many wandering Jews considered Amsterdam the goal of their peregrinations. Polish Jews again worshipped in their own synagogue, as in the second half of the seventeenth century. Their ever increasing stream into the city evoked a prolonged debate in parliament in 1796. One of the members asked bluntly, "What will we do if Jews from Germany and Poland continue to come?"[29] Our list of emigrants shows that about 10 percent settled in Holland at this time.

Emigration to France was now primarily directed toward its northern regions. Information is available regarding immigration to cities such as Metz and Dijon, and various small communities in Alsace. A few Polish Jews also settled in Paris. In southern France the conditions were not favorable for new Jewish immigration; even the Jews of the centuries old Four Communities of Comtat Venaissin had begun to leave their homes for other parts of the country. However, we shall see further on that in spite of these conditions, wandering Jews invaded southern France in this period in large numbers.[30]

A large stream of emigrants moved to England. Already in the 1750s they began to appear in London, dressed in the typical Polish Jewish garb, with beards and sidelocks. This type of immigrant became a common theme for contemporary painters and caricaturists. A Hebrew source, too, relates the presence of "bearded Pollacks" in London. Polish Jews had arrived in such numbers by 1790-1792, that it became necessary for them to establish several *minyanim* (prayer houses), where worship was conducted according to the Polish rite. In 1797 their influx alarmed the Lord Mayor of London, who began to demand, as we have seen, they go back to the Continent or face deportation. At the same time, immigrants from Poland began to appear in provincial communities, such as Falmouth, Dover, Bristol, Portsmouth, Plymouth, and Sunderland, where in 1781 a Polish synagogue was established.[31] The increased immigration to England is reflected in our list of emigrants; about 15 percent made their homes in England.

A number of Polish Jews came to North America in this period. To begin with, in almost all communities of the continent, but mainly in New York and Newport, there were families with the surname Pollack. In most cases it is not possible to determine whether a man bearing this name was a native of Poland or a descendant of one. However it is known that a number of Jews who lived in Charleston, (South Carolina) Philadelphia, Baltimore, Richmond, Newport, (Rhode Island) Easton (Pennsylvania), and New York were born in the Polish commonwealth. Other Polish Jews went to Charleston with the British military forces. In the late 1760s several Jewish families that spoke Polish settled in Philadelphia. In 1770 a Jew who had just arrived from Lissa, and was planning to go on to Jamaica, visited Ezra Stiles in Newport.

In the 1780s a tailor from Poland settled in Charleston with his wife and child. In 1790 poor Jews from Poland arrived in Philadelphia and New York, and asked their congregations for financial help. About half the Polish immigrants known to us arrived before the outbreak of the Revolutionary War and the rest in the last quarter of the century.[32]

More so than in former periods, emigrants from Poland now wandered from place to place in the West before establishing new domiciles. Almost all the Polish Jews who settled in North America spent some time in Holland or England. Many Polish Jews who settled in England had lived first in Germany or Holland. We have seen that the British authorities attributed the arrival of so many alien Jews to the low cost of crossing the channel. Information available about individual emigrants confirms the fact that after leaving Poland, many stayed in the Germanies. We know of emigrants who first settled in Berlin, Altona, Düsseldorf, or the territory of Mecklenburg, and later went to England. The famous *maskil* Solomon Dubno first emigrated to Prussia and then settled in Amsterdam permanently. Zalkind Hurwitz, a native of Lithuania who spent his boyhood in Berlin, went on to Metz and ultimately settled in Paris. Judah Löb Bensew, another *maskil*, spent over a decade in Berlin before making his permanent home in Vienna. It is also worth noting that members of an emigrant family often separated and settled in different countries. Moses Samuel, a native of Krotoschin who became a leading figure in English Jewry, had a sister living in Germany. Of the eight children of Isaac Horowitz, the immigrant rabbi of the tri-community Altona-Hamburg-Wandsbeck, three settled in Germany, Holland, and Moravia, while the others stayed in Poland. These are only a few of many cases that reveal the degree to which Western Europe and North America became a vast "home" for Polish Jews who left their native land. Wandering Jews also covered a much larger area, now reaching England and southern France.[33]

V

Many emigrants who went west during the second half of the eighteenth century were young men who accompanied their families. In a list of Jews living in Berlin around 1810, we find some 20 who came from Poland between 1750 and 1800, and 14 of them were under the age of twenty at the time of their arrival. The others were between twenty and forty. A similar situation is reflected in a list of alien Jews living in Plymouth, England, in 1803. Of the five who were born in Poland, only one was over twenty when they arrived in England.[34] Taking these facts into consideration, one must conclude that many of these immigrants came as youngsters with their parents. These lists were prepared early in the nineteenth century, as noted above; probably by that time the parents had died and therefore were not listed. The available information about individuals confirms that many emigrants were young people. Haym Salomon was in his thirties when he left Poland and the painter Solomon Bennett was thirty-one.[35] It also seems that a considerable number of emigrants first went west alone and were later joined by their families.[36]

In this period, too, emigrants came from all social strata of Polish Jewry. Again an impressive number of rabbis obtained positions in western countries, such as the Germanies, the Hapsburg monarchy, France, and Holland. The brothers Schmelka and Phineas Horowitz, who were appointed to two of the most important rabbinic posts in Europe (Nikolsburg and Frankfort on the Main) in the 1770s, may serve as examples.[37] Many lesser communal functionaries, such as cantors, ritual slaughterers, and *soferim* (scribes), likewise left Poland and obtained positions in the West. That their numbers were large is manifested by the fact that every summer during the annual fair in Frankfort on the Oder there was a "labor exchange" for ritual slaughterers from Poland in search of employment in Germany.

In the Yiddish comedy *Als der Sof iz Gout iz Alles Gout*

(all's well that ends well), when a cantor in Germany is asked to sing, he inquires, "In Polish or German?" We thus see that there were many immigrants from Poland among both cantors and their audiences. Polish cantors could be found in other countries as well. One who was a native of Kalisz lived in the English city of Bristol. A number of famous cantors from Poland held positions in Holland. Scribes from Poland could also be found in various communities in the West. The *Memorbuch* of Bibergau in Bavaria was written in 1771 by a scribe from Lithuania. There were scribes from Poland in London and several Torah readers from Poland were also active there at the same time.[38]

We have seen that there were favorable opportunities for teachers from Poland in most western countries, especially in the Germanies. The sources leave no doubt that numerous teachers made use of these opportunities and emigrated. In Paderborn in western Germany, for example, the influx of Polish teachers was so great that local teachers were in danger of losing their jobs. Seventeen of the 18 men who taught in Bützow in Mecklenburg between 1738 and 1769 were from Poland. In 1772 Levin Joseph, a Jewish educator in Potsdam, estimated that at least 500 Polish teachers were then employed in Prussian lands. In 1782 Hartwig Wessely aptly characterized the situation by observing, "We have become accustomed to having our children raised by teachers from Poland."[39] In addition to the scholars who went west to find employment, many went there to look for support from philanthropic sources. As in former times, many authors emigrated to Germany and Holland for the avowed purpose of publishing and selling their works. Levin Joseph relates that such authors from Poland used all kinds of pressure tactics to sell their works to German Jews.[40] Several mystics from Poland arrived in London at that time and associated with the *Ba'al Shem* (miracle worker) there, also a native of Poland. Solomon Maimon's autobiography shows that a Polish emigrant *maskil* could easily find a wealthy philanthropist eager to help him.[41] An analysis of the occupations of some 130 emigrants reveals that more than 50 percent were intellectuals, such as rabbis, authors, and communal functionaries; the others were mostly merchants and craftsmen. The sources indicate that the proportion of craftsmen in this period was somewhat larger than previously.[42] This situation can be explained by the fact that now the proportion of emigrants from small towns was larger and in small towns Jewish craftsmen outnumbered merchants.[43]

Most of the merchants were peddlers or shopkeepers. Nearly all the Polish Jews living in the territory of Mecklenburg-Schwerin in 1769 were storekeepers. Information available about individuals also shows that storekeepers were well represented among the emigrants. For example, the historian Marcus Jost's father, who immigrated from Jaroslaw to the state of Anhalt, was a storekeeper. Jost relates that his father was a retail merchant who traded at the various fairs. An immigrant retail merchant could also be found in Plymouth, England. The preponderance of shopkeepers and peddlers among the merchants can be explained by the economic structure of the Jewish population of the Polish commonwealth. The number of small shopkeepers (*kramarze, hadlarze, targownicy*) within the merchant class was by far larger than that of businessmen (*kupcy*).[44]

A number of wealthier businessmen could also be found among the emigrant merchants. To be sure, the number of Polish immigrants who came from western regions to the Leipzig fairs was now smaller than previously. However, this was due to a general decline in Jewish participation in the Leipzig fairs during the second part of the eighteenth century.[45] Information about individuals active in business in various western regions is amply available. Most of the Polish immigrants in America in this period were businessmen or owners of factories or plantations. There was a wealthy immigrant merchant in Mecklenburg-Schwerin. Wealthy businessmen could also be found among the Polish immigrants in England and Holland.[46]

96

The problem of wandering Jews now became much more tragic. It was no longer confined to poor immigrants from Poland and Bohemia. The inclination to lead a mobile life prevailed among many people in Western Europe, including German Jews. Even Jews from Turkey now appeared among the wanderers.[47] Yet the sources leave no doubt that still many *Betteljuden* were from Poland. Moreover, definite information is available about the presence of Polish *Betteljuden* in various regions of the West. In 1770 several German states issued severe ordinances against the admission of wandering Jews. They indicated that their actions were prompted by "an epidemic that . . . was spreading over Poland." Several years later the immigration of Jews to Alsace was forbidden for the same reason.[48] It is obvious that most of the wandering Jews in these countries had come from Poland.

Two types of people were represented among the wanderers. While on a journey the Gaon of Vilna wrote to his family that "there are men who go on a long journey for the purpose of collecting money, leaving their wives at home and becoming poor wanderers." The other type of wanderer left Poland with his family and went westward in search of a place that would accept him. A Jewish writer of the time, very much interested in the fate of the wanderers, relates in a pamphlet, *Gedanken über Betteljuden,* that many of them wandered in the vicinity of Würzburg because it admitted them while neighboring territories did not. We will later see that during this period *Betteljuden* were much more widespread over the western countries than previously.[49]

However, now again various types of people could be found among the wandering Jews, and not all were paupers. In 1785 the Prussian government justified its harsh treatment of wandering Jews by claiming they sold wool cloth at the fairs, thus damaging the Prussian textile industry. From this

we can infer that many wandering Jews were in reality peddlers and had brought along merchandise from their homeland. A reliable source relates that the heads of the Jewish
community in Berlin were allowed to admit scholars among
the wandering Jews into the city. That various ecclesiastics,
such as cantors and choristers, also were among the wanderers is clearly stated in *Gedanken über Betteljuden*.[50] However, most of them were undoubtedly paupers without permanent domiciles.

Solomon Maimon relates the reason for his becoming a
wanderer. He went to Germany to study philosophy, but was
denied admission to Berlin and was forced to become a
wandering beggar. "To stay alive," he recounts, "I was compelled to become a vagrant in a strange land." We thus see
that immigrants who arrived in the West for the purpose of
settling in specific places were forced to become *Betteljuden*
when their goals became unattainable. Some wanderers
joined the lower classes of society, thereby causing the Jewish communities in the West much trouble. The comedy *Als
der Sof iz Gout iz Alles Gout* pictures the depravity of these
wanderers. Likewise, *Gedanken über Betteljuden* describes
in detail their physical and moral decay, their apathy and
filth. It also indicates they were quarrelsome and notorious
liars, and were ready to do anything for a small gain. It may
be true that toward the end of the century a number of Polish Jews joined some of the many robber gangs that plagued
the Germanies. Criminals could also be found among the Polish immigrants in England. As early as 1771, about a quarter
of a century before the mass influx of poor Polish Jews, several individuals who may have been Jews from Poland were
sentenced to death in London for robbery and murder.[51]

These unfortunate characteristics of some *Betteljuden* became the more offensive because of the massiveness of their
movement. Many sources that discuss wandering Jews refer
to their large numbers. They were arriving daily and in even
greater numbers before holidays. A writer of the time speaks
of *Bettel-Caravanen* roaming the country. These factors

98

made the problem of wandering Jews a very serious matter. An impression similar to that of a nineteenth century Jewish historian was probably prevalent: the wandering Jews were "a class of the Jewish population in Germany."[52]

The number of wandering Jews in the territories of Prussia was quite large. This is confirmed by official documents as well as other sources. Needless to say, most wanderers were trying to reach Berlin. They gathered at the capital in large numbers, especially during holidays. The government criticized the local Jewish population for aiding the *Betteljuden* and for not stopping their influx. The truth of the matter is, however, that the authorities granted so many special admission privileges to various types of wanderers that it is hardly surprising the ordinances of 1780, 1785, 1788, and 1791 against *Betteljuden* were on the whole ineffective. To begin with, wanderers who were ill or looking for work were allowed to enter Berlin. The authorities also admitted aliens accepted as *domestiques* by *Schutzjuden.* We have also seen that scholars were likewise admitted to Berlin on the recommendations of Jewish communal leaders.[53] It is thus understandable that throughout the second half of the eighteenth century, large numbers of wandering Jews succeeded in entering Prussia.

Wandering Jews could also be found in northern Germany and in Danish territories. It was noted above that they frequently stated their destinations were Altona and Amsterdam. Therefore, it is understandable that upon entering Germany many went northward. Evidence is available about their presence in such regions as Mecklenburg, Hanover, and Hildesheim. The same holds true for Copenhagen and Danish controlled Moisling in the vicinity of Lübeck. In 1763, 1781, 1790 and 1798, severe ordinances were promulgated against them in the bishopric of Hildesheim.

The harshest measures were once again taken by the state of Hanover. Its ordinance of 1770 decreed that "beggars and Polish Jews" were to be barred from the country even when they possessed valid passports. Obviously, the government suspected officials were being bribed to issue passports. It seems the main objective of the ordinance was to detect officials who were helping to smuggle wandering Jews into the country, for it provided that wanderers who refused to name those who assisted them were to be tortured. The punishment to be meted out to a wanderer returning after being deported was to become more cruel with every return. The first time, he was to be thrown into a dungeon for fourteen days. A second return was to be punished by flogging, and the third would draw the death penalty.[54] The cruelty of this ordinance can be explained by the fear of the epidemic raging in Poland at the time. It is also possible the fight Hanover conducted against *Betteljuden* was to prevent them from going on to England, which was united with Hanover under the same ruler.

The situation in southern Germany was not much different. According to reports written at the turn of the century, "large masses of Betteljuden" were living in parts of Bavaria. When barred from certain regions in the country, they gathered in neighboring areas in even larger masses. Some areas had laws which permitted the admission of sick *Betteljuden*. Not all local authorities, however, obeyed these laws.[55] It is safe to assume that the situation was similar throughout the Germanies. On the whole, governments made great efforts to bar wandering Jews who, however, quite often were able to overcome the obstacles and remain in a given territory for some time.

During this period large numbers of wandering Jews were entering France, Holland, and England. The situation that arose in France is illustrated by the following events that took place in the autumn of 1773 in the southern part of the country. Large crowds of *Betteljuden*, among them Jews from Poland, attempted to invade the Four Communities in the Comtat Venaissin. After being denied admission to Avignon, Carpentras, and Cavaillon, they tried to enter Isle-sur-Sorg. About a fourth of them—the sick and women with small children—were admitted. The following day the others again attempted to force their way into the town. The situation became so serious that the Jewish community felt compelled to request protection from the army. Ultimately the wanderers were driven away, but four days later another group of about a hundred *Betteljuden* arrived. The local Jews barricaded their homes and again called in the army from Avignon to protect them from their unfortunate brethren. While all this was taking place in southern France, even larger groups of *Betteljuden* were invading the regions of the country adjacent to Germany—Alsace, Lorraine, and the territory of Metz. In 1790 the city council of Lixheim became alarmed by the "gangs of German, Polish, Turkish, and other Jews who were daily arriving in squadrons."[56] To further illustrate the situation, it is worth noting that by 1797 such a large number of poor Polish Jews had arrived in London that the "Polish" synagogue there suddenly found itself in a precarious financial situation due to the needs of the newcomers.[57]

The survival of the wandering Jews in Western Europe mainly depended on the willingness of Jewish communities to assist them. This fact was well known among the Gentiles and official documents also emphasized it. We have seen that a Prussian ordinance of 1780 blamed the charitableness of local Jews for the influx of *Betteljuden*. The author of *Gedanken über Betteljuden* asserts that every Jew in the Germanies was accustomed from childhood to having *Betteljuden* partake of his meals. Hence the governments of the Germanies took measures to stop the assistance given to wanderers and often succeeded in obtaining the cooperation of Jewish communal authorities in their efforts. Solomon Maimon colorfully described the swiftness with which the overseer of the Jewish poorhouse at the gates of Berlin managed to make him leave the place. An official appointed by the Jewish community of Halberstadt to supervise the movements of *Betteljuden* was directed to treat them harshly. The wardens of the Great Synagogue in London also cooperated with the Lord Mayor in his efforts to deport poor Polish arrivals.[58] In the 1760s when the Ashkenazic community of Amsterdam was about to decide to withhold assistance from alien Jews arriving in the city, Rabbi Saul Löwenstamm, himself an immigrant, dissuaded his community from doing so.[59]

By and large, however, the western governments did not succeed in stifling the compassion the Jews had for their wandering brethren, and communities as well as individuals continued to extend them a helping hand. Jews in Halberstadt often hid wanderers in their homes to protect them from the overseers. Even the group of wanderers who tried to force their way into the Four Communities in southern France in 1773 were given alms. This is all the more significant in view of the fact that at that time the once prosperous Jewry of southern France was already experiencing economic decline.

Gedanken über Betteljuden describes in detail the aid Jewish communities in the region of Würzburg were giving *Betteljuden*. The tiny Jewish community of Gochsheim of only 26 families issued 1,650 "billets" a year, each one entitling a wanderer to a day's stay with a local family. The cost to the community ran as high as 350 florins. The Jewish communities of the region annually issued a combined total of 68,000 billets. The community of Schnaitach distributed as many as 10,000 billets to wanderers each year. The pamphlet stresses the fact that the aid given to wanderers by the Jews of other regions was equal to that given in the region of Würzburg, and at times even surpassed it. The communal officer in charge of issuing billets was popularly known as the *Plettengabbe*.[60]

The system of persecution followed by governmental agencies did not solve the *Betteljuden* problem. Neither did the assistance given by Jewish communities appreciably improve the situation. *Betteljuden* were becoming a permanent part of the Jewish population and their numbers were now so large that various people began to search for a more humane and lasting solution. At the end of the eighteenth century many men in the Germanies were concerned with the idea of improving the lot of the poor. Against this background the pamphlet mentioned above, entitled in full, *Gedanken über Betteljuden und ihre bessere und zweckmässigere Versorgung* (*On a Better and More Useful Treatment of Beggar Jews*), was written by a Jewish book dealer, Joseph Isaak of the town of Gochsheim. It was published in Nuremberg in 1791 and was dedicated to Francis Ludwig, duke of Franconia and bishop of Bamberg and Würzburg, whom Isaak considered a great humanitarian. He gives a description of the *Betteljuden* living in the region at the time which, as we have seen, was a distressing picture of moral and physical decay. We further learn from the pamphlet that in the district of Franconia, discussions took place regarding possible solutions to the *Betteljuden* problem. Isaak apparently wrote his pamphlet to influence these discussions; in its latter part he offered some concrete suggestions toward a solution. His main suggestion was to establish special workshops for some wanderers, while others were to be given work as water carriers and wood choppers (compare Joshua 9: 27). Women were to be employed as spinners and nursemaids. He also suggested that schools should be established to give the children a free education. In addition, he submitted plans for raising the funds necessary to implement his program. It seems, however, that Isaak's plan was never carried out. In 1803, twelve years later, Franz Oberthür, a Catholic theologian, revived Isaak's suggestions for solving the problem of wandering Jews, still present in the region of Würzburg "in large masses." He proposed in addition that a hospital be built for the old and sick. We thus see that when the eighteenth century was drawing to a close, neither Jewish society nor the governments of western countries were making any substantial progress toward a solution to the problem. The nineteenth century inherited the serious problem of wandering Jews, whose numbers reached their highest peak at that very time. It would be many decades before the wandering

Jews were to be integrated within the Jewish population of Western Europe and become *geachtete Bürger ihrer Heimat* (respected citizens of their countries).[61]

VII

The precise number of Jews who left their homes in Eastern Europe to go west during the second half of the eighteenth century is not known. The general impression obtained from the sources is that their number was larger than in former periods. Much of the information justifying this impression is given above. At this point, however, several of these facts should again be emphasized. To begin with, many emigrants who went west took their families. Moreover, it has been shown that during this epoch the average Polish Jewish family numbered five or six persons.[62] Another fact to be considered is that when fairly accurate statistics are available about certain groups of emigrants, for example teachers, their numbers were very large. Further evidence that emigration was continuing on a large scale is implicit in the fact that during the eighteenth century the center of the Jewish population of the Polish commonwealth moved eastward even more than in the preceding century.[63] We have seen that during a 200 year period, it was mainly Jews from the western provinces of the commonwealth who participated in the migratory movement to the West. It should therefore be safe to assume that the sharp decline in the Jewish population of western Poland during the eighteenth century was due mostly to emigration to Western Europe rather than to migration to eastern parts of the commonwealth.

The information available about the numbers of Polish immigrants in the German states is rather limited. In regard to Prussia, only a few details can be ascertained. The lists of the Jewish inhabitants of Berlin show only some 20 families from Poland.[64] However, the literary sources reveal that the actual number from Poland was much larger. There is no reason to doubt the accuracy of the statement of the renegade teacher Levin Joseph that 500 alien Jewish teachers were employed in Prussia in 1772. This number does not appear exaggerated in view of the fact that three of Lazarus Bendavid's five teachers and 17 of the 30 *melamdim* in Breslau were Polish Jews.[65] Even though many teachers were unmarried, and some who were married had left their families in Poland, it is reasonable to assume that in Prussia, Polish teachers and their relatives together constituted an immigrant group of at least 1,000. We also can get an idea of the number of Polish Jews in Silesia by analyzing statistical data on Breslau. Of some 500 Jewish families in the city, about 170 were from Poland, constituting almost 35 percent of the Jewish population. Moreover, it seems that some of the Jews who came from the two old communities of Glogau and Zülz were originally from Poland.[66] Apparently the Polish Jewish immigrant population in Silesia was quite large, and most likely totaled several thousand. Certain statistics are also available regarding Königsberg. A list of 255 Jews who died there between 1770 and 1810 names at least 105 who can positively be identified as having been born in Poland. Using this as a basis for an estimate of the composition of the Jewish community, we may infer that about 40 percent of Königsberg's Jewry during the second half of the eighteenth century were from Poland. True, it is possible that some of those listed immigrated to the East Prussian capital before 1750 and that others came to seek medical aid rather than to settle permanently. However, this is balanced by the fact that others in the list may have come from Poland, although they cannot be identified as such. Considering all these possibilities, we may conclude that a large part of the 855 Jews living in Königsberg at the turn of the century emigrated from Poland between 1750 and 1800.[67]

Mecklenburg-Schwerin is the only northern German state where fairly accurate statistics on Polish immigrants are available. In the 1760s a list was prepared of all the Jews living there. This list, which contains detailed information on origins and occupations, was published by Olaf Gerhard Tychsen of the University of Bützow.[68] In 1769, 195 Jewish families lived in 31 localities. Of these families, 36 can be identified as immigrants from Poland, constituting at least 18 percent of the total Jewish population. Besides the immigrants in the official list, a considerable number of teachers from Poland were employed in Mecklenburg-Schwerin.[69] There is no way of knowing their exact number, because teachers often changed their locations and were not counted among the permanent Jewish population.

It is impossible to make an exact estimate of the number of Polish Jews who settled in western and southern Germany in this period, because relevant information is extremely scarce. If the names assumed by the Jews of Baden in 1809 were to be considered the only valid source of information, we would conclude that very few were from Poland.[70] Only 4 percent of the names indicate foreign origin, their bearers coming from Poland, Bohemia, Austria, and Switzerland. But the few available literary sources tell an entirely different story. When Rabbi Hirsch Janów of Posen went to Germany to become rabbi of Fürth and was joined by most of the students of his yeshivah, the group must have included at least 30 or 40 persons.[71] No doubt, there were several hundred nonconverted Polish Jews among the 800 Frankists that settled in Offenbach with their master Jacob Frank.

Although the information offered by the sources is so meager, we must still assume that a large number of Polish Jews settled in the Germanies. Because the limitations on Jewish marriages imposed in many states were still largely in force, they greatly cut down the natural increase of the Jewish population. An additional decrease resulted from conversions to Christianity. Although conversion among German Jews did not become a mass movement, it did remove a sizable number from the Jewish fold.[72] Considering all this, we have to assume that the increase of the Jewish population in the Germanies during this period was to a large degree due to immigration, with Polish Jews still the most conspicuous group. Taking for granted that at midcentury the Jewish population in the Germanies totaled some 65,000,[73] and that by the end of the eighteenth century it rose to 200,000,[74] we have to conclude that many, many thousands of Polish Jews had immigrated during the second half of the century. In the same period, a substantially smaller number of immigrants settled in the western parts of the Hapsburg monarchy. There is no way of arriving at any concrete figure.

Nor are figures available on the emigrants who went to Holland. We will again have to assume that several thousand entered the country during this period. According to one estimate, the Ashkenazic community of Amsterdam doubled in size between 1748 and 1780, rising from 10,000 to 19,000 souls, and grew by an additional 2,000 in the next fifteen years.[75] It is hard to say whether these statistics are sufficiently valid for estimating the number of Polish Jews who immigrated to the city. But in any case, the estimate that between 1780 and 1795 the Ashkenazic community grew by only 2,000 will have to be disputed, for at this time deputies in the Batavian parliament complained about the great influx of Jewish immigrants from Germany and Poland. Be that as it may, it is certain that the growth of the Jewish population in Amsterdam, which made it the largest Jewish community in Europe, should be partly ascribed to the arrival of several thousand Jews from Poland.

There is no way of accurately determining the number of Polish immigrants to France and England during this half century. As for France, we have to stress the fact that government circles were alarmed by the influx of Jews from Germany and Poland, and one official put Poland at the head of the list of countries of origin.[76] Various estimates were made of the size of the Jewish population in England. One contemporary estimate at the end of the eighteenth century put the number at 12,000, another at 26,000. According to additional calculations, London's Jewish population trebled in this period as a result of immigration. At this time several

Polish synagogues were established in London, and in the new synagogue in Sunderland, worship was conducted according to the Polish rite.[77] From all this we may conclude that the increase in England's Jewish population was largely the result of immigration from Poland.

We can make a better estimate of the number of Polish Jews who settled in North America in this period. We find in various lists about a dozen names of immigrants from Poland, both single and family men.[78] Since there were probably immigrants from Poland who have not yet been identified as such, we may conclude that there were close to 100 Polish Jews in the United States around the time of the founding of the Republic.

VIII

The number of wandering Jews was very large during this period in the Germanies and other western European countries. Official documents, such as the Prussian ordinance of 1780 against wanderers, repeatedly stress their large numbers. To be sure, officials who tried to keep wanderers out of their territories may have exaggerated their numbers. Likewise, we cannot be sure they were as numerous as the Jewish communal authorities claimed. *Betteljuden* were a great social and financial burden to the Jewish communities, and there was a tendency to overstate their numbers. The pamphlet *Gedanken über Betteljuden* states the Jewry of the Würzburg region was convinced that from 8,000 to 9,000 *Betteljuden* were sojourning in the vicinity. Its author himself was of the opinion these numbers were exaggerated. In 1803, however, trustworthy Jewish and non-Jewish sources refer to great numbers of wanderers. Professor Oberthür of Würzburg speaks of the presence of "large masses" of *Betteljuden* in the vicinity of the city. Similarly, Marcus Jost tells in his memoirs, as we saw, that when he was ten years old many scholars from Poland passed through his home town

108

of Bernburg in the territory of Anhalt.[79] We thus see that although the complaints of the governments and of the Jewish communal authorities may have been exaggerated, there was a widespread belief that wanderers were coming to Germany in large numbers. We might therefore question the figure of 1,000 wanderers for all Franconia given by *Gedanken über Betteljuden* as too small.[80]

Yet we cannot disregard Joseph Isaak's assertion, since it was based on an analysis of various data and was not a mere impression. We may perhaps go a step further and try to use this number, with reservations, as a starting point for an estimate of the total number of wandering Jews in the Germanies. We already have stressed that they must have sojourned mainly, and perhaps exclusively, in areas where Jewish communities existed. If we accept Isaak's assertion that in the Würzburg region, with a permanent Jewish population of 5,000 (1,000 families), there were about 230 wanderers,[81] and if we assume that the proportion between the permanently settled and wandering parts of the Jewish population was approximately the same everywhere in the Germanies, we may then figure that in addition to a stable Jewish population of about 200,000 there was a wandering one of about 10,000. It is impossible, of course, to say whether this figure is correct, but it can be said with certainty that the number of wanderers was not less than 10,000. Of course, not all wandering Jews were from Poland. Moreover, the proportion of Polish Jews among the wanderers was smaller during the second half of the eighteenth century than in preceding periods. Considering all this, we may safely say that at least 5,000 Polish *Betteljuden* sojourned at this time in the Germanies. Since this period stretches over five decades, and the mortality rate among wanderers was extremely high, we may arrive at the conclusion that during the second half of the eighteenth century at least 10,000-15,000 Polish Jews of the lower and poorer classes left Poland for the Germanies, where they remained as wanderers the rest of their lives.

We also have some inkling of the number of wandering

Jews in France. The "invasion" of the Four Communities in southern France in 1773 was carried out by two groups of *Betteljuden*, each numbering about 100 people. The bulk of French Jewry, however, lived in the northern parts of the country, in Alsace, Lorraine, and Metz and vicinity, and the *Betteljuden* in all likelihood sojourned mainly in the northern provinces. The city council of Lixheim in Lorraine complained in 1790, as we have seen, that "squadrons" of *Betteljuden* were arriving daily.[82] Whether this was an exaggeration or not, we will have to assume that there, too, groups of wanderers appeared, each numbering about 100.[83] It may therefore not be incorrect to infer that during these fifty years, thousands of classless and poor Jews, probably half of them from Poland, entered French territories. As for Holland and England, we have to be satisfied with the assertion that the poor Jews who came in during this period were "large in numbers."[84]

IX

Practically all the emigrants from the Polish commonwealth to the West in this period remained in their adopted homelands for the rest of their lives. In many cases it is possible to identify their progeny as inhabitants of various localities in western countries. Only a few returned to Poland, and now too, they were mostly sons of rabbinic families who obtained rabbinic positions in the old country.[85] Immigrants generally made genuine efforts to become an integral part of their local Jewish as well as non-Jewish society. The son-in-law and biographer of Rabbi Raphael Cohn describes how his father-in-law acquired friends during his first visit to Germany and how they later helped him to obtain the important position as rabbi of the tri-community of Altona-Hamburg-Wandsbek. We find similar descriptions in the autobiography of Solomon Maimon. More than other emigrants, Maimon stressed the fact that once a man settled in the West, he could not consider the idea of going back to Poland. When Maimon's wife came to Breslau to demand his return to Lithuania or a divorce, the great philosopher chose what he called the "lesser of two evils"—a divorce. "I had now lived in Germany some years," he said, "had happily emancipated myself from the fetters of superstition and religious prejudice, had abandoned the rude manner of life in which I had been brought up, and had extended my knowledge in many directions. I could not return to my former barbarous and miserable condition, deprive myself of all the advantages I had gained . . ." And he understandably tried to persuade his son, who had accompanied his mother, to remain in Germany.[86]

Following the great influx of *Betteljuden* from Poland to the West, the nickname Pollack assumed a more derogatory connotation than ever before.[87] Nevertheless, we know of many cases of immigrants who married into local Jewish families, including the aristocracy. We find various instances of such "intermarriages" in the lists of Berlin Jews of this period. It is worthwhile to describe a number from other localities, too. After the death of Hirsch Janów, the rabbi of Posen and Fürth so highly praised by Solomon Maimon, his widow, a daughter of an immigrant rabbi, married the rabbi of Dessau, Michael Speier, a German. The late rabbi's daughter likewise married a Jew from Halberstadt. An immigrant from Posen who lived in Offenbach married a daughter of a German Jew from Bingen. Some of the Polish Jewish immigrants in the state of Mecklenburg married women who lived in small towns there.[88] The case of Rabbi Benjamin of Krotoschin is noteworthy. He first served as rabbi of Obornik in western Poland and in 1759 became rabbi in Hanau. His first wife was a native of Wronki, a town near Posen. His second wife, however, was a native of a small town in Germany. One of his daughters married the rabbi of Gelnhausen. The other daughter became the wife of the rabbi of Hanover, Mordecai Baer Adler, a native of Frankfort on the Main. Their son Nathan Adler served as chief rabbi of the British

Empire.[89] Besides the immigrant rabbis who married into rabbinic families in the West, a considerable number of immigrants married into the Jewish lay aristocracy. The following are a few examples. The daughter of a Polish rabbi, who immigrated to Fürth in 1789, married the leader of its Jewish community. A Jew from Lissa, who lived in a small town in Mecklenburg, married the daughter of a court-Jew. The son of the rabbi of Cleves, an immigrant from Poland, married a woman of the aristocratic Gomperz family. Moses Samuel, an immigrant from Krotoschin who acquired an enormous fortune in England, married a daughter of a German court-Jew, who was also his brother-in-law, the husband of his sister.[90]

The successful efforts of Polish immigrants to become integral parts of western Jewish society represent only one side of the picture. There also existed many tensions between immigrant and native Jews. In addition, much as in former times, immigrants tended to retain their separate Eastern European identity. One has the impression that these tendencies were even stronger than in former periods. The separate Polish synagogues that had been founded in Breslau around a century earlier were still flourishing. Much emphasis was put on conducting the services according to the rites of Poland and Lithuania. When Saul Löwenstamm, the immigrant rabbi of Amsterdam, died in 1790, the Polish Jews who until then had prayed in his private chapel established a separate synagogue. This synagogue was to serve solely the religious needs of Polish Jews, and the communal authorities agreed to its establishment on condition German Jews would not be permitted to worship there. We have seen that several Polish *minyanim* (prayer houses) were established in the 1790s in London, and that in the Sunderland synagogue services were conducted in accordance with the Polish rite.[91] In Amsterdam a separate neighborhood of Polish Jews existed at the end of the century.

Cases of name changing were now rather rare. True, here and there we find immigrants changing their names, as for

112

instance Trina, the daughter of an immigrant rabbi in Fürth, who changed her name to Teresa. Generally, however, they seem to have shunned name changing. This becomes apparant when we analyze lists of Polish immigrants in Berlin, in Plymouth, England, and in North America. Practically none of them had given up his Jewish name, even in public life.[92]

The separateness of the immigrants was both a source and a symptom of tensions that existed between the two parts of the Jewish population in the West. Perusal of the literary sources conveys the impression that now these tensions were stronger than in the first half of the century. These were the times when efforts began to be made for emancipating the Jews, especially in the Germanies. The widespread slogan was that the time had come when all differences between Jews and Christians ought to disappear. It was natural, therefore, that the arrival of many "bearded Pollacks" in their long garb was disturbing. In the Yiddish comedy *Als der Sof iz Gout iz Alles Gout*, a Polish Jew becomes very angry when he thinks a respected German Jew wants him to shave off his beard.[93] In England, where the immigration of "bearded Pollacks" brought into the country a hitherto unknown type of Jew, the newcomers were given a none too friendly welcome. Solomon Bennett, the artist from Lithuania, wrote that the Jews of London openly discriminated against their co-religionists who did not speak German, French, or Italian.[94] It is obvious that he referred to immigrants from Eastern Europe.

Certain categories of Polish immigrants encountered opposition among western Jews because they were potential competitors in the professions. We have seen that in the preceding generation Jacob Emden complained that Polish rabbis obtained the best rabbinic positions in the Germanies. Now, too, we encounter a similar case. Simon of Geldern, Heinrich Heine's notorious uncle, complained in his diary that the Polish scholars in the Germanies were conceited and considered themselves unsurpassed in learning. He probably blamed the competition of Polish rabbis for failures in his own career. Complaints that Polish teachers took bread away from native teachers were heard in Paderborn, as we have seen. Animosity toward immigrant competitors explains an anecdote, popular among German Jews in the early years of the nineteenth century, which described a successful immigrant from Poland as "deceitful in business."[95] The tension between native German Jews and immigrants, especially poor wandering Jews, is depicted in blazing colors in *Als der Sof iz Gout iz Alles Gout*. It is hard to determine whether the anonymous author was a German Jew, but it is certain he did not have much liking for immigrants. The types of Polish Jews introduced in the comedy are all outspokenly negatives—swindlers, wife deserters, ignoramuses, and the like. Lippmann, the representative German Jew, however, is a fine man with a gentle heart. Although he is magnanimous and always ready to help, the "Pollacks" try his patience so much that he, too, begins to hate them. The reaction of the Polish immigrants to this seemingly universal animosity is represented in the person of Yoksh. He heaps many insults upon Lippmann and calls the average German Jew an "ignoramus." He tries to "prove" his point in a curious manner, saying that the word *Ashkenaz* (German) is composed of the first letters of the Hebrew words *anashim shefalim kelavim noafim zolelim* (vile and unchaste individuals, dogs and gluttons).[96] The picture obtained from the comedy vividly recalls the tension that prevailed between German Jews and Polish immigrants about 120 years earlier, as portrayed in the poem *Die Beschreibung fun Ashkenaz un Polack*. The comedy shows that the tension was much more serious around the close of the eighteenth century than during the second half of the seventeenth.

Along with these tensions and the tendency of immigrants to retain their former identity, a strong process of westernization constantly took place among them. Although there were "bearded Pollacks" in England, other immigrants were quite eager to change their appearance and dress. This is clearly shown by portraits of Polish immigrants which have

114

been preserved. Moses Samuel, who arrived in England at the beginning of this period, and the artist Solomon Bennett, who arrived at its close, were both shaved, wigged, and dressed in western garments. Mordecai Cohen, the Zamosc born richest man of South Carolina, was equally westernized in appearance.

We have seen that in general Polish immigrants quickly learned to speak the languages of their new homelands. In this period, moreover, some of them acquired a much deeper knowledge of western tongues. We are told that Rabbi Raphael Cohn of Altona-Hamburg-Wandsbek attained so thorough a knowledge of German that he could distinguish between good and poor styles. Ezekiel Landau, the renowned immigrant rabbi of Prague, knew German equally well. Immigrant *maskilim* quite naturally were the first to acquire a thorough knowledge of western languages. Israel Samosch conducted a series of philosophical dialogues with the German scholar Christoph Friedrich Nicolai that appeared in print in 1753. Hartwig Wessely reports that non-Jewish scholars in Germany befriended the *maskilim* who arrived from Poland and admired their erudition. The ingenious philosophical works in German by Solomon Maimon, the treatise on the Jewish question written in French by Zalkind Hurwitz, and a book in Dutch by Judah Littvak give ample evidence of the achievements of *maskilim* in mastering western languages. We have an interesting example of linguistic integration in the renegade physician-poet Issachar Baer Falkensohn. He went to Germany from Zamosc in 1767 at the age of twenty-one, and learned German so quickly and thoroughly that four years later he was able to publish a volume entitled *Gedichte eines polnischen Juden* (German poetry by a Polish Jew). In Britain, too, Polish immigrants wrote works in English. Examples are artist Solomon Bennett's books and polemical pamphlets. As for the United States, historians of early American Jewry stress the fact that in this period immigrants, including those from Poland, underwent a process of rapid Americanization.[97]

Together with linguistic integration, a desire to participate in public life began to grow among the Polish immigrants in the countries of their western dispersion. The following illustrate this. Twenty-three natives of Poland, who had arrived in Berlin before 1800, were among the 300 Jewish inhabitants of the Prussian capital to obtain the much-coveted municipal citizenship at the turn of the century. In the United States a Polish Jew was a member of the Supreme Council of Scottish Rite Masonry in 1801.[98] Even better examples are the careers of several other Polish emigrants. The most famous, of course, was Haym Salomon, whose role in the American Revolution has often been exaggerated. Whatever his actual contribution may have been, the fact remains that the Jew closest to the Founding Fathers was an immigrant from Poland.

In Western Europe, too, the revolutionary movements beginning in 1789 paved the way for political activity by immigrants from Poland. Two men earned special distinction in this respect. In Paris it was Zalkind Hurwitz. He was born into a rabbinic family in Kovno and in his youth studied Torah in Lithuania. He became active in the popular movement to improve the situation of the Jews in Poland. While still there he published in a Warsaw newspaper a refutation of an anonymous attack on the Jews. Like many others, he lost his hope for a better Jewish lot in Poland and left for the West. He first went to Berlin, where he associated with the Mendelssohn circle. Later he went farther west, first to Metz, and then to Paris, where he lived in great poverty as an old clothes dealer. However, when a position at the Royal Library became vacant, Hurwitz was appointed to it. With the outbreak of the French Revolution, he joined the National Guard and contributed one fourth of his salary to the Republic. Among the revolutionaries Hurwitz distinguished himself as a radical and published courageous articles in the French press, in which he attacked the reactionaries and fought for Jewish equality. He wrote one of the most significant works of the epoch on the Jewish question, *Apologie des Juifs,* published in Paris in 1789. In this work, which was awarded a prize by the Royal Society of Arts and Sciences in Metz, Hurwitz identified himself as a Polish Jew.[99]

Judah Littvak belonged to the same category. As his name indicates, he too was a native of Lithuania. Like Hurwitz, as a young man he immigrated to Berlin and became a member of the *maskilim* circle. He was learned in mathematics and later became a teacher of this subject in Holland. When the Batavian Republic was established there, Littvak was active in the organization of the radical political club, *Felix Libertaté.* In 1807 he served as a delegate of Dutch Jewry to the Sanhedrin in Paris.[100]

X

The religious and cultural impact of immigrants on Jewish communities in the West was of the utmost importance. We have seen that without the *melamdim,* rabbis, and other religious functionaries from Poland, western Jewry would probably have been unable to maintain its spiritual and religious existence. The situation was similar in the area of the more modern type of Jewish education that began to emerge in the West. Polish immigrants were, as we have already seen, a very important group among the *maskilim.* It will suffice to mention here four men in the *Haskalah* movement in the West—Isaac Satanów, Solomon Maimon, Judah Löb Bensew, who was active in Berlin and Vienna, and Shalom Hakohen, active in Germany, Holland, Austria, and England. Hartwig Wessely justly praised the Polish *maskilim* for the erudition they had acquired while still in the old home: "And we have seen among our brethren from Poland . . . men great in learning, who studied in their homeland, without the help of teachers, the disciplines of geometry and astronomy, and they attained in these sciences such a deep knowledge that non-Jewish scholars wondered how they could have achieved this without the help of teachers."[101] From the circles of these *maskilim* came the more modern educators who contributed to the growth of a new type of Jewish education in Western Europe. Such an educator was Faivish Horowitz, a Polish *maskil* who went to The Hague, where he became a teacher and published a Yiddish textbook in mathematics. Another was Hyman Hurwitz, who followed his father from Poland to England and founded a modern Jewish school in London, the Highgate Academy. He was later appointed instructor of Hebrew at the University of London. Gedaliah Moses, a native of Obersitzko in western Poland, served as a principal of Jewish schools in Scandinavia, first in Stockholm, subsequently in Copenhagen.[102] These facts show how Jewish education in the West, both traditional and modern, was largely dependent on teachers from the Polish commonwealth.

As was pointed out above, Polish rabbis held many positions in western countries. Moreover, some of the most important rabbinic posts were occupied by immigrants all through the second half of the century. The three scholars who were successively rabbis of Frankfort on the Main during this period, Jacob Joshua, author of *Penei Yehoshua*, Abraham of Lissa, and Phineas Horowitz, came from Poland. It is noteworthy that whenever this community needed to elect a rabbi, primary consideration was given to Polish candidates. After Joshua's death the three candidates put on the ballot were Polish rabbis. At the next election, two of the three candidates were from Poland. The tri-community Altona-Hamburg-Wandsbek also continued to favor Polish scholars as rabbis. Isaac Horowitz and Raphael Cohn, two of the four men who held this position during the half century, were Polish scholars. The community of Metz likewise was headed by two Polish rabbis. The most famous of the emigrant rabbis was Ezekiel Landau, who was called from Jampol to be rabbi of Prague in 1754. The story of his career there for thirty-eight years is well known. His activities were of a much wider scope than those of a religious leader; often he exercised the political leadership, not only of the Jewish

118

community in Prague, but of the entire Jewish population in the Hapsburg monarchy.[103]

As in former times, sons of immigrant rabbis held many rabbinic positions in western countries, often inheriting those of their fathers. For example, a son of Rabbi Schmelka of Nikolsburg occupied various rabbinic positions in Moravia. Rabbi Hirsch, the son of Rabbi Phineas of Frankfort on the Main, who had come to Germany to head a yeshivah, succeeded his father as rabbi of Frankfort. Asher, a son of Rabbi Aryeh Löb of Metz, inherited his father's position, after holding rabbinic posts in the Germanies. Samuel Landau, the son of the rabbi of Prague, at first taught at his father's yeshivah. After his father's death, he was appointed to the rabbinic court, and following a prolonged struggle became its president.

Other immigrant rabbis established "dynasties" in the West, whose members held important posts during the entire nineteenth century. Descendants of Rabbi Levi Saul Löwenstamm held the most important rabbinic positions in Holland uninterruptedly for 150 years. A rabbinic dynasty was established in Germany by Salomon Kohn, who became rabbi of Fürth in 1789 after holding rabbinic positions in western Poland and Silesia. His son and grandson were both rabbis in communities in Germany throughout the nineteenth century. As we have seen, another immigrant rabbi, Benjamin of Krotoschin, was the ancestor of two chief rabbis of the British Empire. Many rabbis in Germany were also his descendants.[104]

An impressive number of immigrants achieved socioeconomic advancement in the West. Most of the Polish Jewish immigrants in the United States were active in important business enterprises. Haym Salomon's contacts with leaders of the American Revolution resulted from his financial transactions. That an immigrant from Zamosc, Mordecai Cohen, became the wealthiest man in South Carolina has already been mentioned.[105] Cases of Polish immigrants who achieved great wealth are also known in Western Europe.

In Amsterdam, for instance, we find a Jew from Vilna who succeeded in accumulating a fortune. The often mentioned Moses Samuel, who died at the age of ninety-seven, was born in Krotoschin and arrived in England as a young man. He first dealt in old clothes in London's rag fair, but later became one of the wealthiest Jews in the country. Other Polish immigrants also amassed considerable wealth in London.[106]

Much information is available about the economic success of Polish immigrants in the Germanies. Here and there we find individuals who became wealthy. One was Judah Moses of Darguhn, in the duchy of Mecklenburg, who came from Birnbaum in Poland. A Polish Jew who went to Berlin, possibly before 1750, was chosen by the "sector of the rich" as an elector of the communal administration in 1762, and another Polish Jew became an elector in 1777. A picture of the economic success of Polish immigrants in Berlin can be obtained from an analysis of various lists in Berlin's *Judenbürgerbücher*. They give the occupations of 19 Jews from Poland, who arrived in the city as adolescents, and whose economic activities thus had begun after that. Among them we find 5 bankers, 2 manufacturers, 9 merchants, one dentist, one teacher, and one tailor. The striking economic rise of many immigrant youths is reflected in this occupational list.[107]

It was natural that economic success helped some immigrants to gain acceptance among the upper classes of western Jewry. We shall see further that, as in former periods, immigrants now also played significant roles in the leadership of Jewish communities. In addition, members of that new immigrant group, the *maskilim*, were readily admitted to the upper classes of Jewish and also to some extent Gentile society, regardless of their economic status. The desire to acquire knowledge was so strong in the West that scholars were generally accepted, much like humanists during the Renaissance. When we read Solomon Maimon's autobiography and Hartwig Wessely's description of the relations between Polish *maskilim* and Gentile scholars and scientists, it becomes apparent that the former attained a truly high status in western society.[108]

Another aspect of the integration of Polish immigrants in the West is the role some of them played in philanthropy and communal leadership. Sometimes programs of organized self-help were started by the immigrants themselves. It was mentioned above in another connection that when large numbers of poor Polish Jews arrived in London in 1797, the Polish synagogue gave them such extensive aid that it ran into financial difficulties. Individual emigrants were responsible for many charitable deeds. For example, a Jew in Königsberg left part of his property to support poor Jews in Lissa. We may, of course, suppose that he came from Lissa and remembered its poor when preparing his will. A native of Shklov, who lived in Breslau, donated a curtain for the Holy Ark of the Schklower Schul (synagogue) in Breslau. In England we find among the immigrants men who contributed to charity on a large scale. Simon Solomon, a native of Lissa who died in London in 1817, was a generous philanthropist. The greatest of all the philanthropists of the time was Moses Samuel. He made it possible for London's Ashkenazic community to acquire a site for a new cemetery, and he built a synagogue in the resort town of Bath, where he used to spend his summers. When he died in 1839 he left large amounts for various worthy causes. Among others, he endowed London's Great Synagogue with the then considerable sum of £1,500 to provide clothes for the poor every year before Passover. At the turn of the century we encounter the first great philanthropic act of a Polish immigrant in the United States. A contemporary writer reports as follows: "In the Common Year 1800, Meyer Polony, a native of Poland died in New York, and bequeathed to the Congregation [Shearith Israel] the sum of $900, the interest to be applied towards the establishment of a Hebrew School."[109]

We also find Polish immigrants active in communal institutions. They were members of various Jewish organizations, such as the Gesellschaft der Brüder in Breslau and the burial society in Königsberg. In London they were among the wardens of the Great Synagogue. In various communities, for example, Copenhagen and localities in Mecklenburg, Polish immigrants were elected *parnasim* (elders). In Berlin, too, they were chosen for important positions, such as electors of the communal administration and *gabaim* (trustees) of funds collected for the Holy Land and of other charities. In this period an immigrant was even elected an elder of the community, an honor never before attained by a Polish Jew in Berlin. He was one of two immigrants identified in communal documents as belonging to the "sector of the rich," and held the office of elder during the last two decades of the eighteenth century. In 1791 Moses Clava Levy, a merchant who was born in a small town near Cracow, served as president of Congregation Beth Elohim in Charleston, South Carolina.[110] Thus economic success placed some Polish immigrants in the highest honorary positions of the Jewish communities. Election to the office of elders symbolized the highest degree of integration into a Jewish community an immigrant could attain.

XI

Having traveled a long way in our efforts to present a picture of the westward migrations of Jews from Eastern Europe, we now can discern certain distinct patterns that were characteristic of the entire movement. To begin with, all social classes of Eastern European Jewry participated. We have also seen that scholars were always proportionately the largest group among emigrants. It is possible the sources mislead us to a certain degree, because in an age when statistical data were all but nonexistent, a rabbi or a scholar stood a better chance of being "immortalized" in the sources than an ordinary man. The degree of possible error, however, is limited. It is a fact that both the Jewish communities and individual Jews in the West were more willing to extend a helping hand to the scholar than to the ordinary man among the immigrants. It is also true that the western communities were in great need of the services of scholars, rabbis, and other communal functionaries, while an influx of merchants from Poland was liable to create competition for permanent Jewish residents.[111] To a certain degree the situation resembled the recent immigration policy of the United States, which favored the immigration of clergymen and scholars. We are therefore correct in supposing that the picture obtained from the sources, which reveals a very large proportion of intellectuals among the emigrants, is by and large accurate. Emigrants of the lower classes, possessing neither knowledge nor financial means, usually had no choice but to become wandering Jews.

Another very important characteristic of the movement is the proportion of emigrants from western Poland and Lithuania, the provinces adjacent to Germany, was much higher than from the central and eastern provinces of the commonwealth. The reasons for this phenomenon were discussed in detail above and here it is only necessary to stress its great importance.

Of the countries that became the destinations of the emigrants, it should be said in conclusion that during the entire period of 200 years, all the lands—from Austria in the south and East Prussia in the north to the far distant Americas in the west—had a part in absorbing them. And yet, although Holland and England were at times centers of great attraction, it was Germany that received the bulk of the emigrants. One of the reasons for this should be repeated here: the long common border between the Polish commonwealth and Germany facilitated emigration. Another reason undoubtedly lies in the fact that Yiddish speaking emigrants could understand and learn German more easily than Dutch, French, or English. Many emigrants realized, after their arrival in Germany, that for a variety of reasons it could not become their new home. They then went on to other western countries. The number of individuals whose migratory careers developed along these lines was so large that one can only consider this phenomenon an important pattern in the entire movement. It should be pointed out, however, that when migration by sea was possible, Holland became the primary destination.

That the available data fail to give a clear picture of the numbers of the emigrants is indeed disappointing. The only consolation lies in the fact that the fragmentary information offered by the sources, which have been discussed in great detail, leaves no doubt that the numbers involved were very large. Emigrants had a great share in the numerical growth of Jewish settlements in western countries during the nineteenth century. Their significance becomes even clearer when we consider that all through the nineteenth century large numbers of Jews left Germany and the Hapsburg monarchy for America. In addition, German Jewry lost a certain number of converts to Christianity. If German Jewry nevertheless numbered in the hundreds of thousands, it was at least partly a result of the influx of Jews from Eastern Europe during the seventeenth and eighteenth centuries. The fact that in 1933 Dutch Jewry numbered more than 100,000—Amsterdam's Jewish proletariat numbered in the tens of thousands —was also at least partly due to the influx of Polish Jews during these two centuries. This has been clearly recognized by Dutch Jewish historians.[112]

The westward migration of Jews from Eastern Europe in the nineteenth century possibly played an even greater role in the growth of Western Europe's Jewry than the movements of the preceding two centuries. However, the partitions of Poland in the last decades of the eighteenth century resulted in the annexation of large parts of the commonwealth by Prussia and Austria. The westward migratory movement of Eastern European Jewry in the nineteenth century, therefore, presents a quite different picture from that of the preceding two centuries and should be dealt with separately. Another major desideratum of Jewish historiography would be to describe in detail what the descendants of the Eastern European immigrants of the seventeenth and eighteenth centuries contributed to Jewish and general culture in the western countries during the great *Sturm und Drang* epoch of the nineteenth century.[113] A new look at the history of the Jews in western countries in the last 150 years from the vantage point of the migratory movements described above may lead us to a deeper understanding of the true historical character of this epoch and of its Jews.

Abbreviations

AJHQ	American Jewish Historical Quarterly
BJGL	Blätter für jüdische Geschichte und Literatur
EJ	Encyclopaedia Judaica
H	*in Hebrew*
Hazofeh	Hazofeh Lehokhmath Israel
HJ	Historia Judaica
JE	The Jewish Encyclopedia
JFF	Jüdische Familien-Forschung
JGJCR	Jahrbuch der Gesellschaft für Geschichte der Juden in der Czechoslovakischen Republik
JJGSH	Jahrbuch für die jüdischen Gemeinden Schleswig-Holsteins
JJLG	Jahrbuch der Jüdisch-Literarischen Gesellschaft
JQR	The Jewish Quarterly Review
JSS	Jewish Social Studies
MGDJ	Mitteilungen des Gesamtarchivs der deutschen Juden
MGWJ	Monatsschrift für Geschichte und Wissenschaft des Judentums
MJHSE	The Jewish Historical Society of England: Miscellanies
MZJV	Mitteilungen zur jüdischen Volkskunde
PAJHS	Publications of the American Jewish Historical Society
REJ	Revue des Études Juives
TJHSE	The Jewish Historical Society of England: Transactions
Y	*in Yiddish*
ZGJD	Zeitschrift für die Geschichte der Juden in Deutschland

Notes

See list of abbreviations. Note numbers for previously cited works, usually in same chapter, are in brackets; colons precede page or verse numbers.

INTRODUCTION

1. R. Mahler, *Toledoth Hayehudim Bepolin* [H] (Merḥavyah 1946): 93-94.
2. In a dramatic poem, *Die Beschreibung fun Ashkenaz un Polack* [Y] [Description of the German Jew and the Polish Jew] (Publications of the Yiddish Scientific Institute, *Studies in Philology* 3 [1929]: 540-51), c. 1675 (see M. Weinreich, ed.: 538), a Polish Jewish immigrant in Germany tells German Jews who are unfriendly to him that when they escaped to Poland because of the war, they were received by their co-religionists in a much friendlier manner (545). The decision of the Lithuanian Council of Provinces of 1639 to care for 57 "Jewish boys who left their homes and came from far away naked, without clothes, and barefooted" probably also refers to refugees from Germany (*Pinqas Hamedinah* [H], ed. S. Dubnow [Berlin 1925]: 73).
3. L. Lewin's "Deutsche Einwanderungen in polnische Ghetti" (JJLG 4 [1906]: 293-329; 5 [1907]: 75-154) admittedly mainly portrays a situation created by the eastward migrations of Jews from Germany to Poland before 1648 (145-46).
4. See *Ashkenaz un Polack* [n. 2].
5. Beth Hillel on *Yoreh De'ah* [H], ch. 201, par. 36 (I was told that certain scholars who came to Hamburg as refugees from Vilna in 1656 introduced this custom). For influence of Polish Yiddish on Dutch Yiddish, see *Reshumoth* n.s. 1 (1946): 120-29.
6. A. Grotte, *Deutsche, Böhmische, und Polnische Synagogentypen* (Berlin 1915): 63.
7. H. I. Bloom, *The Economic Activities of the Jews of Amsterdam in the Seventeenth and Eighteenth Centuries* (Williamsport, Pa. 1937): 110 n. 127.
8. W. W. Kaplan-Kogan, *Die Wanderbewegungen der Juden* (Bonn 1913).

9. F. Bloch, *Die Juden in Militsch* (Breslau 1926). F. Koeltzsch (*Kursachsen und die Juden in der Zeit Brühl's* [Leipzig 1928]: 12) also noticed that during 18th cent. Jews returned to some German cities that had expelled them in 16th. Cf. S. Dubnow, *Weltgeschichte des jüdischen Volkes* 7 (Berlin 1928): 13; S. W. Baron, *A Social and Religious History of the Jews* 2 (New York 1937): 171-72.

10. The importance of the picture obtained from sources at my disposal lies in the fact that it represents rather *less* than what really happened.

11. C. Roth, *A History of the Jews in England* (Oxford 1941): 155 n. 1.

12. M. H. Stern, *Americans of Jewish Descent* (Cincinnati 1960).

13. E.g., Gabriel Eskeles, native of Cracow, was rabbi first in Prague, then Metz, and ultimately chief rabbi of Moravia in Nikolsburg. See *Die Juden und Judengemeinden Mährens in Vergangenheit und Gegenwart*, ed. H. Gold (Brünn 1929): 46.

14. See intro. to his *Present Reign of the Synagogue of Duke's Place* (London 1818): 2-3; the French Revolution prevented his going to Paris to settle.

15. That emigrants from Poland were overwhelming majority of *Betteljuden* can be assumed from the fact that the combined Jewish population of Bohemia and Moravia in mid-18th cent. was slightly more than 10,000 families (*Jahrbuch für die Geschichte der Juden und des Judentums* 4 [1869]: 223-24), while Poland's Jewish population then is estimated at 750,000 (Mahler [n.1]: 233).

16. The futility of German governments' efforts to stop immigration of itinerant Jews is demonstrated by endless number of ever harsher ordinances against them issued throughout 18th cent.

17. For curious stories of eternal wanderers, see Koeltzsch [n. 9]: 201; *Yeshu'oth Zaddiqim* [H] (Warsaw 1905): 3. For vivid descriptions of large groups of *Betteljuden*, see S. Posener, "The Social Life of the Jewish Communities in France in the 18th Century," JSS 7(1945): 222-23.

18. See Posener [n. 17]; H. Conrad, ed., *Das Juden-Buch des Magister Hosmann*, 2d ed. (Stuttgart 1919): 128, 137 (Jews from Eastern Europe in gang of much feared robber Nickel List). There is an extensive literature on 18th cent. German *Gaunertum* (underworld). See also Koeltzsch [n.9]: 203-4.

19. S. Haenle (*Geschichte der Juden im ehemaligen Fürstenthum Ansbach* [Ansbach 1867]: 133) said *Betteljuden* were "eine Klasse der jüdischen Bevölkerung in Deutschland," and "I could name some descendants [of *Betteljuden*] who are now among the most respected members of their community" (138).

20. J. Shatzky, *Gezeires Takh* [Y] (Vilna 1938): 91*.
21. Bloch [n. 9]: 9.
22. In a list of Jews living in duchy of Mecklenburg in 1769 (JFF 2 [1925-26]: 119-71) most immigrants from Eastern Europe came from western Poland, only a few from central Poland, and none from the Ukraine.
23. Roth [n.11]: 233.
24. The widespread belief that the 1881 pogroms were responsible for large scale emigration of Russian Jews to America, which began at that time, seems to be contradicted by the fact that Jews emigrated from Galicia, where pogroms did not take place, in about same proportion as from Russia. See A. Ruppin, *Soziologie der Juden* 1 (Berlin 1930): 133.
25. Cf. W. Sombart, *The Jews and Modern Capitalism* (London 1913): 22-60; F. Priebatsch, "Die Judenpolitik des fürstlichen Absolutismus im 17. und 18. Jahrhundert," *Forschungen und Versuche zur Geschichte des Mittelalters und der Neuzeit, Festschrift Dietrich Schäfer* (Jena 1916): 564-651. Variety of attitudes and inconsistencies is eloquently described by S. Stern in *Der Preussische Staat und die Juden* (Berlin 1925). Lately the problem has been reexamined by M. Arkin in HJ 22 (1960): 85-104. As early as 1577 William I of Orange negotiated with Jews in Frankfort/Main re possibility of admitting Jews into Antwerp. Cf. *Zion* n.s. 15 (1950): 93-106.
26. Stern [n. 25].
27. A. Ackermann (*Geschichte der Juden in Brandenburg* [Berlin 1906]) gives no info. on immigrants from Eastern Europe.
28. R. Kestenberg-Gladstein in *Zion* n.s. 9 (1944): 3-4 n.11.
29. Koeltzsch [n. 9]: 10, 369-70. This was due, of course, to policy of powerful minister, Count Brühl (1733-63), who was friendly to idea of Jewish settlement.
30. See Z. H. Ilfeld, *Divrei Negidim* [H] (Amsterdam 1799): 20b; Roth [n. 11]: 233; S. Posener in JSS 1 (1939): 291.
31. M. Balaban, *Die Judenstadt von Lublin* (Berlin 1919): 56.
32. R. Berndt, *Geschichte der Juden in Gross-Glogau* (Glogau n.d.): 42.
33. "Illegal" Jews often became fictitious "servants" of rich Jews to be permitted to live in various cities and towns. Some wealthy Jews had several families with as many as 100 people on their "payroll." See M. Stern (JJLG 19 [1928]: 66) for how Jewish communities in Germany created a multitude of communal "jobs" to gain right for certain Jews to stay in their towns; he lists more than 20 such "positions" in mid-18th cent. Berlin (n. 1).

34. Kestenberg-Gladstein [n. 28] lists many communities in which censuses of Jewish populations were taken and limitations imposed on number of Jewish families.
35. This is evident from data collected by Lewin [n. 3].

CHAPTER ONE

1. H. P. Stokes, *Studies in Anglo-Jewish History* (Edinburgh 1913): 209; *Die Juden und Judengemeinden Mährens in Vergangenheit und Gegenwart*, ed. H. Gold (Brünn 1929): 343.
2. JE 5: 192; 6: 465.
3. See testimonies in *Pene Yehoshu'a, Even Ha'ezer* [H], par. 63.
4. Ibid., par. 66; Zemaḥ Zedeq [H], par. 108.
5. S. U. Günzburg's *Mar'eh Hamussar* [H] (Offenbach 1716), quoted in S. Assaf, *Meqoroth Letoldoth Haḥinukh Beisrael* [H] 4 (Tel Aviv 1948): 228. First ed. of *Mar'eh Hamussar* was publ. in Prague (1614).
6. H. Kellenbenz, *Sephardim an der unteren Elbe* (Wiesbaden 1958): 78.
7. Dr. jur. Victor, *Die Emanzipation der Juden in Schleswig-Holstein* (n.p. n.d.): 5; EJ 6: 1115.
8. I. Schwarz, *Das Wiener Ghetto* (Vienna 1909), esp.: 198 ("Abrahamb Polackh Hoff Judt"). See also M. Balaban in ZGJD n.s. 4 (1932): 1. The fact that many immigrants were named Polack shows they or their fathers were recent arrivals, most probably in early decades of cent.
9. *Pene Yehoshu'a, Even Ha'ezer*, pars. 63, 65.
10. Ibid., par. 63.
11. Schwarz [n. 8]: 185, 188, 209, 214.
12. Cf. lists in M. Ginsburger, "Wandernde Juden zur Zeit des Dreissigjährigen Krieges," *Jahrbuch der Gesellschaft für die Geschichte der Israeliten in Elsass-Lothringen* (Gebweiler 1917): 11-27.
13. J. Buxtorf, *Judenschul* (Basel 1643): 619. See Y. L. Zlotnik (*Midrash Hameliẓah Ha'ivrith* [H] [Jerusalem 1938]: 22-23) for sources of this epigram. Dr. Dov Yarden kindly called this citation to my attention.
14. Analysis of origin of c. 30 emigrants in a list I compiled from various sources; it also indicates their destinations in Germany.
15. R. Mahler, *Toledoth Hayehudin Bepolin* [H] (Merḥavyah 1946): 94.
16. *Pene Yehoshu'a, Even Ha'ezer*, par. 63. See also S. Hock, *Die Familien Prags* (Pressburg 1892).

17. M. Hendel, *Mela'khah Uva'aley Mela'khah Be'am Israel* [H] (Tel Aviv 1955): 191.
18. H. I. Bloom, *The Economic Activities of the Jews of Amsterdam in the Seventeenth and Eighteenth Centuries* (Williamsport, Pa., 1937): 130; A. Wiznitzer, *Jews in Colonial Brazil* (New York 1960): 107, 109, 189 n. 33.
19. Judah Löb Polack d. 1657 in Vienna, where a child of his d. 1648 (B. Wachstein, *Die Inschriften des alten Judenfriedhofs in Wien* 1 [Vienna 1912]: 272). See also Schwarz [n. 8]: 185, 188, 215.
20. A scholar who returned from Germany to Poland was Jacob Koppelmann of Brześć Kujawski, author of a famous commentary to *Sefer Ha'iqqarim* [H]. See H. N. Dembitzer, *Keliloth Yofi* [H] 2 (Cracow 1893): 88b.
21. *Zemaḥ Zedeq*, par. 108; Wachstein [n.19]. For a case of name changing, which always indicates integration, see Ginsburger [n. 12]: 14 (Polish *Betteljude* named *Philipp* in Alsace).

CHAPTER TWO

1. Cf. N. Hanover, *Abyss of Despair*, tr. A. J. Mesch (New York 1950).
2. See above [intro. n. 2].
3. "A Seventeenth Century Autobiography," in A. Marx, *Studies in Jewish History and Booklore* (New York 1944): 183.
4. See JFF 2 (1935): 719-22.
5. Hanover [n. 1]: 64.
6. M. Balaban in *Beth Israel Bepolin* [H] 1 (Jerusalem 1948): 89.
7. F. Bloch, *Die Juden in Militsch* (Breslau 1926): 4.
8. S. Stern, *Der Preussische Staat und die Juden* (Berlin 1925) 1, pt. 2: 151.
9. Balaban [n. 6]: 88.
10. *Ma'asei Tuvyah* [H] (Lemberg n.d.), pref.
11. H. I. Bloom, *The Economic Activities of the Jews of Amsterdam in the Seventeenth and Eighteenth Centuries* (Williamsport, Pa., 1937): 66-67; F. Priebatsch, "Die Judenpolitik des fürstlichen Absolutismus im 17. und 18. Jahrhundert," *Forschungen und Versuche zur Geschichte des Mittelalters und der Neuzeit, Festschrift Dietrich Schäfer* (Jena 1916): 592-93.
12. S. Stern, *The Court Jew* (Philadelphia 1950): 219-27.
13. *Emunath Shemuel* [H] (Lemberg 1884), par. 10.
14. See above [intro. n. 2].

15. Stern [n. 8] 1, pt. 1: 51, 54. See A. Kohut (*Geschichte der deutschen Juden* [Berlin n.d.]: 548) for earlier permits of this type.
16. H. Kellenbenz, *Sephardim an der unteren Elbe* (Wiesbaden 1958): 194.
17. S. Gronemann, *Genealogische Studien über die alten jüdischen Familien Hannovers* (Berlin 1913): 122.
18. JJLG 7 (1909): 185-86.
19. I could not obtain 1st ed.; ed. of 2d ed. was Jacob Koppel ben Z'ev of Jaroslaw.
20. This booklet is not easily available either; my sources are *Ozar Hasefarim* [H]: 116; Y. Raphael, *Rishonim W'aharonim* [H] (Tel Aviv 1957): 179-81.
21. Hanover [n. 1]: 121.
22. *Die Memoiren der Glückel von Hameln*, ed. D. Kaufmann (Frankfort/Main 1896): 36.
23. JJLG 7 (1909): 172, 185-86.
24. *Hazofeh* [H] 8 (1924): 291, 294; Bloom [n. 11]: 25-26.
25. Moses Rivkes in intro. to *B'er Hagolah* [H], *Tur Orah Hayyim*, quoted by S. M. Hones, *Toledoth Haposqim* [H] (Warsaw 1910): 56.
26. L. Müller, "Aus fünf Jahrhunderten: Beiträge zur Geschichte der jüdischen Gemeinden im Riess," *Zeitschrift des Historischen Vereins für Schwaben und Neuburg* 26 (1899): 129.
27. I. Kracauer, *Geschichte der Juden in Frankfurt am Main 2* (Frankfort/Main 1927): 45, based on entry in community minutes book. This shows Rivkes was not well informed when he wrote, "Also in the community of Frankfort they did the refugees many favors" [n. 25]. The almost complete absence of names indicating Polish origin on Frankfort's Jewish cemetery's gravestones of the last half of 17th cent. is additional proof refugees were not admitted (see M. Horowitz, *Die Inschriften des alten Friedhofs der israelitischen Gemeinde zu Frankfurt am Main* [Frankfort/Main 1901]).
28. Priebatsch [n. 11]: 581, 583; Stern [n. 8] 1, pt. 1: 35-37.
29. Stern, ibid.: 45, 67, 68, 72; pt. 2: 31, 151, 154, H. Jolowicz, *Geschichte der Juden in Königsberg* (Posen 1867): 16-17.
30. K. A. Schaab, *Geschichte der Juden in Mainz* (Mayence 1854): 227, 241; *Zion* n.s. 9 (1944): 4 n. 11; H. Bodemeyer, *Die Juden: Ein Beitrag zur Hannoverschen Rechtsgeschichte* (Göttingen 1855): 18.
31. See Priebatsch [n. 11]: 620; F. Baer, *Das Protokollbuch der Landjudenschaft des Herzogtums Kleve* (Berlin 1922): 62 n. 234; Bloch [n. 7]: 5-6; Stern [n. 8] 1, pt. 2: 4-5.
32. See S. Haenle, *Geschichte der Juden im ehemaligen Fürstenthum*

Ansbach (Ansbach 1867): 108; Müller [n. 26]: 112-13; MJHSE
1 (1925): xxv-xxxiii.
33. Stern [n. 8] 1, pt. 2: 4-5.
34. Hanover [n. 1]: 64-68; N. Brüll, *Ḥazon Nahum* [H] (Cracow
1892): 71.
35. *Beth Israel Bepolin* [n. 6]: 86.
36. Gershon Ashkenazi, *Avodath Hagershuni* [H] (Frankfort/Main
1699), par. 36; *Maasei Tuvyah*, intro.; Brüll [n. 34].
37. S. Carlebach (*Geschichte der Juden in Lübeck und Moisling*
[Lübeck 1898]: 11-12) states, e.g., Moisling's Jewish community
was founded by refugees from Chmielnicki riots in the Ukraine,
yet he cites as his source a memorial prayer recited in Moisling
that lists solely rabbis of communities in vicinity of Posen (n. 1).
This, of course, proves beyond doubt Moisling immigrants came
in 1655. A similar error was made by J. C., ed. of minutes book
of Portuguese Jewish community in Hamburg (see JJLG 7
[1909]: 173 n. 1).
38. *Die Juden und Judengemeinden Mährens in Vergangenheit und
Gegenwart*, ed. H. Gold (Brünn 1929): 206, 225, 281, 332, 421.
39. Ibid.: 592.
40. Hanover [n. 1] is only contemporary author who seemingly
speaks of large numbers of 1648 refugees who fled to Germany.
It should be remembered, however, he did not go to Germany
himself, and as his info. is probably from hearsay, it cannot be
considered valid in comparison with local sources. Equally unreliable is chronicle *Sh'erith Israel* [H] (Nowy Dwor 1785):
78b ("boatloads" of Polish Jews arrived in Amsterdam already
in 1648), written c. 80-90 years later. Lithuanian order of prayer
was followed by "Polish" synagog in Amsterdam in latter 17th
cent. (see doc. publ. by I. D. Markon [*Ziyunim* (H) (Berlin 1929):
179], showing synagog was founded by Lithuanians who could
not have arrived before 1655). Bloom ([n. 11]: 25-26), indeed,
lists sources reporting arrival of Polish and Lithuanian Jews in
Amsterdam in 1655-56 and also quotes Jan Wagenaar, 18th
cent. Dutch author, that hundreds of Polish Jews fled to Amsterdam in 1654, "after the Cossack uprising under Chmielnicki."
This late source is probably unreliable too. Had there been
several hundred Polish Jews in Amsterdam before arrival of
Lithuanians, their synagog would not have adopted Lithuanian
minhagim (religious customs). The possibility should be considered that Lithuanians began to flee as early as 1654 after
Moghilev on the Dnieper surrendered to Muscovite army and
its Jews were ordered out. See S. M. Dubnow, *History of the
Jews in Russia and Poland* 1 (Philadelphia 1916): 153.
41. Glückel [n. 22; see also nn. 23-24].

42. D. Kaufmann, *Die letzte Vertreibung der Juden aus Wien* (Vienna 1889): 62 n. 1.
43. Bloch [n. 7], *pass.*; *Tit Hayawen* [H], ed. J. Gurland (Cracow 1892): 18.
44. JJLG 6 (1908): 158-59.
45. *B'er Hagolah*, intro.; Stern [n. 8] 1, pt. 2: 151.
46. *Beth Israel Bepolin* [n. 6]; ZGJD n.s. 4 (1932): 5.
47. The 3 "West Polish" synagogs were those of Jews from Krotoschin, Lissa, and Kalisz. Cf. M. Brann, "Etwas von der schlesischen Landgemeinde," *Festschrift zum siebzigsten Geburtstage Jacob Guttmanns* (Frankfort/Main 1915): 232 n. 2; L. Lewin, *Die Landessynode der grosspolnischen Judenschaft* (Frankfort/Main 1926): 37.
48. B. H. Auerbach, *Geschichte der israelitischen Gemeinde Halberstadt* (Halberstadt 1866): 60; J. Shatzky in *Yivo Bleter* 10 (1936): 252; Bloom [n. 11]: 54.
49. Gronemann [n. 17]: 7; A. Eckstein, *Geschichte der Juden im ehemaligen Fürstbistum Bamberg* (Bamberg n.d.): 160-62; JJLG 8 (1910): 139-40; HJ 12 (1950): 147-48; REJ 8 (1884): 260 f.; E. N. Adler, *London* (Philadelphia 1930): 100-1.
50. See *'Emunath Shemu'el* [H], par. 52. Case is described in question signed "Hillel, rabbi of Hamburg," probably none other than author of *Beth Hillel*, rabbi there, 1670-80 (see E. Duckesz, *Iwoh Lemoschaw* [H] [Cracow 1903]: 6).
51. J. Picciotto, *Sketches of Anglo-Jewish History*, rev. & ed. I. Finestein (London 1956): 50.
52. See Stern [n. 8] 1, pt. 2: 529-30; J. B. Koenig, *Annalen der Juden in den deutschen Staaten, besonders in der Mark Brandenburg* (Berlin 1912): 129; JFF 12 (1936): 721; M. Freudenthal, *Aus der Heimat Mendelssohns* (Berlin 1900): 118, 283, 284; E. Landshuth, *Toledoth 'Anshei Hashem Ufeulatham Baadath Berlin* [H] (Berlin 1884): 55.
53. E. M. Fuchs, *Über die ersten Niederlassungen der Juden in Mittelfranken* (Berlin 1909): 23.
54. J. Emden, *Megillath Sefer* [H] (Warsaw 1896): 5; *Zemah Zedeq* [H], par. 101.
55. My lists collected from various sources have only a limited value, of course, as these sources are to a certain degree incidental; nevertheless, they reflect general situation and strongly corroborate results obtained from systematic perusal of other sources.
56. *'Emunath Shemu'el*, par. 10.
57. Jolowicz [n. 29]; Stern [n. 8] 1, pt. 2: 154.
58. Ibid., pt. 1: 139.
59. Ibid.; JFF 3 (1927): 528; Glückel [n. 22]: 217-18.

60. A. Levy, *Geschichte der Juden in Sachsen* (Berlin 1900): 56;
    L. Löwenstein, *Geschichte der Juden in der Kurpfalz* (Frankfort/
    Main 1895): 132. See also above [intro. n. 29].
61. Freudenthal [n. 52]: 37, 117, 271. In 1688 a Jew named Polack
    went from Bernburg to Leipzig fair. See idem, *Leipziger Mess-
    gäste* (Frankfort/Main 1928): 44.
62. Emden [n. 54]: 11; Carlebach [n. 37]; 2, 26, 29; JJGSH 6 (1934-
    35): 35.
63. Bloom [n. 11]: 26; Löwenstein [n. 60]: 131.
64. JJLG 6 (1908): 157 ff., 167; Fuchs [n. 53]; L. Lamm, *Zur Ges-
    chichte der Juden in Lauingen* (Berlin 1915): 47-49; H. Barbeck,
    Geschichte der Juden in Nürnberg und Fürth (Nuremberg
    1878): 39.
65. Gold [n. 38], *pass.*; Hanover [n. 1]: 121; Bloch [n. 7]: 40-41;
    Priebatsch [n. 11]: 619 n.5; Emden [n. 54]; JGJCR 1 (1929):
    95, 111, 149; S. Hock, *Die Familien Prags* (Pressburg 1892).
66. I. Elbogen, *Geschichte der Juden in Deutschland* (Berlin 1935):
    144; *Festschrift* [n. 47]: 225 ff.
67. Bloch [n. 7]: 9, 14; *Beth Israel Bepolin* [n. 6]; *Festschrift* [n.
    47]: 242, 245, 247 (Jonathan Bloch of Cracow and Solomon of
    Graetz near Posen, ancestors of Gratz family of Philadelphia);
    JFF 11 (1935): 678-712.
68. B. Brilling, *Geschichte der Juden in Breslau von 1454 bis 1702*
    (Stuttgart 1960): 68-71; JFF 3 (1927): 506; *Festschrift* [n. 47];
    E. Hintze, *Katalog . . . der Ausstellung "Das Judentum in der
    Geschichte Schlesiens"* (Breslau 1929): 22.
69. *Abhandlungen zur Erinnerung an Hirsch Perez Chajes* (Vienna
    1933): 247 ff.; I. Schwartz, *Das Wiener Ghetto* (Vienna 1909):
    225, 237, 249, 250; J. Taglicht, *Nachlässe der Wiener Juden*
    (Vienna 1917): 162.
70. *B'er Hagolah*, intro.; Bloom [n. 11]: 25 n. 113, 66, 67; *Ziyunim*
    [n. 40]: 159-80; S. J. Finn, *Qiryah Ne'emanah* [H] (Vilna 1915):
    100, 133; EJ 7: 749; J. Shatzky, *Gzeires Takh* [Y] (Vilna 1938):
    88*-89*.
71. *Ma'asei Tuvyah* [H], intro.; C. T. Weiss, *Geschichte und recht-
    liche Stellung der Juden im Fürstbistum Strassburg, besonders
    in dem jetzt badischen Teile, nach Akten dargestellt* (Bonn
    1896): 39; *Festskrift I Anledning Af Professor David Simonsens
    70-Aarige Fodselsdag* (Copenhagen 1923): 284; JSS 7 (1945):
    214.
72. See F. Guggenheim-Grünberg, "Die ältesten jüdischen Familien
    in Lengnau und Endingen," *Schweizerischer Israelitischer
    Gemeinde Bund: Festschrift zum 50 jährigen Bestehen* (Zurich
    1954): 126, 128, 129; idem, *Die Sprache der Schweizer Juden
    von Endingen und Lengnau* (Zurich n.d.): 12 (there were 4

named Polag among 28 Jewish families in Endingen c. 1750; these Polags were known to have large families).

73. C. Roth, *A History of the Jews in England* (Oxford 1941): 155 n. 1; Adler [n. 49]; Picciotto [n. 51]; MJHSE [n. 32]. A Lithuanian Jew reached Dublin before 1700 (see C. Roth, *Anglo-Jewish Letters* [London 1938]: 87; Kellenbenz [n. 16]: 69).

74. Even a community like Frankfort/Main that refused to admit 1656 refugees, usually admitted rabbis and scholars from Poland (see Horowitz [n. 27]).

75. Cf. above [nn. 10, 17, 46, 49, 54, 70].

76. *Ashkenaz un Polack* [intro. n. 2]: 541.

77. Gronemann [n. 17]: 7, 122; Emden [n. 54]: 11.

78. *Ashkenaz un Polack* [intro. n. 2]: 541, 547; Bloom [n. 11]: 66-67, 119; Glückel [n. 22]: 75, 218; Freudenthal [n. 52]: 14, 118; idem [n. 61], *pass.*

79. Bloom [n. 11]: 41.

80. *Ashkenaz un Polack* [intro. n. 2]: 546. Most local studies on Jewish communities deal with settlement tax Jewish immigrants had to pay.

81. Müller [n. 26]: 112-13; MJHSE [n. 32].

82. Müller [n. 26]: 129.

83. Carlebach [n. 37]: 18.

84. Name Polack usually indicated bearer was immigrant from Poland or son of one.

85. Stern [n. 8] 1, pt. 1: 140 n. 11.

86. E.g., Freudenthal [n. 52]: 14, 118, 283-84; Eckstein [n. 49]; JJLG 6 (1908): 167.

87. S. Stein, *Geschichte der Juden in Schweinfurt* (Frankfort/Main 1899): 46; Carlebach [n. 83].

88. E. Shulman, *Sefath Yehudith-Ashkenazith Vesifruthah* [H] (Riga 1913): 46.

89. Priebatsch [n. 11]: 592.

90. Gold [n. 38]: 112, 123, 173, 184, 206, 225, 235-36, 281, 289, 295, 302, 317, 332, 388, 421, 517-18.

91. *Ziyunim* [n. 40]: 166.

92. Bloom [n. 11]: 31; *Sura* [H] 3 (1957-58): 293.

93. Letter by Josiah Pardo, Sephardic rabbi of Amsterdam (*Hazofeh* 8 [1924]: 295). It is possible, of course, not all immigrants from Poland belonged to Polish community. If, however, 400 constituted 20 percent of Ashkenazic population, one would be inclined to question Bloom's assertion [n. 92] that there were c. 5,000 Ashkenazim in Amsterdam in 1674.

94. I. M. Zunz, *'Ir Hazedeq* [H] (Lemberg 1874): 125.

95. *'Emunath Shemu'el,* par. 1.

96. See, e.g., JJLG 8 (1910): 78, 139-40; *Jubelschrift Hildesheimer* (Berlin 1890), H sect.: 85; Freudenthal [n. 52]: 284, 298; D. Weinbaum, *Geschichte des Friedhofs in Dyhernfurth* (Breslau 1903): 5 n. 1; Gold [n. 38]: 6, 185, 370; Marx [n. 3]; Schwarz [n. 69]: 225, 237.
97. *Ashkenaz un Polack* [intro. n. 2]: 544; Glückel [n. 22]: 75, 90; Zunz [n. 94]: 124; JJLG 6 (1908): 169-70; Duckesz [n. 50]: 18; Gronemann [n. 17]; Gold [n. 38]: 370.
98. Bloom [n. 11]: 29; Freudenthal [n. 52]: 284.
99. *Ashkenaz un Polack* [intro. n. 2]. That this poem was publ. twice in a short time demonstrates acute tension (538).
100. For Polish community in Amsterdam and its "constitution," see Markon [n. 40]: 159-80; see also *Kelilath Yofi* [H] 1: 96b. For attempt to enlist intervention of Council of the Four Lands, see I. Maarsen (*Hazofeh* 8 [1924]: 289, 293-99), citing letters to council from Amsterdam's Sephardic community; it is hard to imagine Sephardim would have written them without knowledge and consent of Polish community.
101. Freudenthal [n. 52]: 37; Carlebach [n. 37]: 11-12, 28.
102. EJ 7: 749.
103. Freudenthal [n. 52]: 28; Glückel [n. 22]: 90.
104. Freudenthal [n. 52]: 28, 298; A. Jellinek, *Märtyrer- und Memorbuch* (Vienna 1881): 16.
105. Weinbaum [n. 96].
106. Bloom [n. 11]: 56; Freudenthal [n. 52]: 117, 235 ff.
107. Bloom [n. 11]: 41, 66, 67; *Festskrift* [n. 71]: 254.
108. See above [nn. 101, 103]; *'Emunath Shemu'el*, par. 10.
109. E.g., Wahl family in Dessau (see Frudenthal [n. 52]: 118), or Alexander Polack, wealthy Amsterdam money changer, 1674 (see Bloom [n. 11]: 176 n. 9).

CHAPTER THREE

1. A. Shohet, *Beginnings of the Haskalah among German Jewry* [H] (Jerusalem 1960).
2. 'Avi 'Ezri Margalioth, *Ḥiburei Liqutim* [H] (Amsterdam 1715): 5b.
3. 'Eli'ezer Lifschitz, *Heshiv Rabbi 'Eli'ezer* [H] (Neuwied 1749), intro.
4. See, e.g., S. M. Dubnow, *History of the Jews in Russia and Poland* 1 (Philadelphia 1916): 167-87; R. Mahler, *Toledoth Hayehudim Bepolin* [H] (Merḥavyah 1946): 290-357.

5. M. Balaban, *Die Judenstadt von Lublin* (Berlin 1919): 55-60.
6. His *Rosh Yosef* [H] (Cöthen 1717), intro.
7. Z. Horowitz, *Kithvei Hage'onim* [H] (New York 1959): 31.
8. B. H. Auerbach, *Geschichte der israelitischen Gemeinde Halberstadt* (Halberstadt 1866): 53.
9. J. H. Simchowitz in MGWJ 54 (1910): 616.
10. His *N'ta Sha'ashu'im* [H] (Amsterdam 1735), intro., quoted by A. Yaari, *Mehqerei Sefer* [H] (Jerusalem 1958): 111.
11. S. Stern, *Der Preussische Staat und die Juden* (Berlin 1925) 1, pt. 2: 408-9; 2, pt. 2: 330; *Meqom Shemu'el* [H] (Altona 1738), intro.
12. J. Emden, *Megillath Sefer* [H] (Warsaw 1896): 110; 'Elyaqim of Komarno, *Melamed Siah* [H] (Amsterdam 1710), intro., quoted by S. Asaf in *Meqoroth Letoldoth Hahinukh Beisrael* [H] 1 (Tel Aviv 1926): 183-84; *Kelilath Yofi* [H] 2: 89b. How Emden could write on his visit to Poland in 1718 that "there scholars earn their livelihood easily and with dignity" (70) is hard to explain. When he wrote this many decades later, he must have idealized situation in Poland when he was young.
13. See Shohet [n. 1]: 21-33.
14. Emden [n. 12]: 77.
15. *Hiburei Liqutim* [n. 2]: 2a.
16. Stern [n. 11] 2, pt. 2: 12-14, 96; S. Haenle *Geschichte der Juden . . . Ansbach* (Ansbach 1867): 91, 158; H. Barbeck, *Geschichte der Juden in Nürnberg und Fürth* (Nuremberg 1878): 82; JJLG 19 (1928): 40.
17. According to official Berlin police lists (MGDJ 2 [1910]: 58), Jewish families there increased from 180 in 1728 to 350 in 1749; Jewish population of Prussia as a whole also almost doubled during same period. See also J. B. König, *Annalen der Juden in den deutschen Staaten, besonders in der Mark Brandenburg* (Berlin 1912): 233, 256; H. Jolowicz, *Geschichte der Juden in Königsberg* (Posen 1867): 52, 56; J. Jacobson, *Jüdische Trauungen in Berlin 1723-1759* (Berlin 1938): 12-13; G. Liebe, *Das Judentum in der deutschen Vergangenheit* (Leipzig 1903): 78; Stern [n. 11] 2, pt. 1: 10, 11, 24; pt. 2: 95, 330, 336, 360, 375, 526, 714, 718. Decree of 1722 was directed against Jews from other German states as well, not esp. against Polish Jews.
18. J. Meisl, ed., *Protokollbuch der jüdischen Gemeinde Berlin (1723-1854)* (Jerusalem 1962), *pass.*, esp.: 77-85, 120-29; Stern [n. 11] 2, pt. 2: 335.
19. JJLG 19 (1928): 40; König [n. 17]: 230.
20. *Festschrift zum siebzigsten Geburtstage Jacob Guttmanns* (Frankfort/Main 1915): 228; R. Berndt, *Geschichte der Juden*

in *Gross-Glogau* (Glogau 1873): 42; Liebe [n. 17]: 80; JGJCR 1 (1929): 184, 199, 236; *Die Juden und Judengemeinden Mährens in Vergangenheit und Gegenwart*, ed. H. Gold (Brünn 1929): 14.

21. A. Levy, *Geschichte der Juden in Sachsen* (Berlin 1900): 56, 65, 76; F. Koeltzsch, *Kursachsen und die Juden in der Zeit Brühls* (Leipzig 1928): 10.

22. K. A. Schaab, *Geschichte der Juden in Mainz* (Mayence 1854): 282, 344; Barbeck [n. 16]: 57; A. Lewin, *Geschichte der badischen Juden* (Karlsruhe 1909): 51; R. Hallo, *Geschichte der Familie Hallo* (Kassel 1930): 90 (4 Polish *melamdim* were living in Kassel).

23. Dr. jur. Victor, *Die Emanzipation der Juden in Schleswig-Holstein* (n.p. n.d.): 8; MGJV 22 (1907): 46.

24. Jacobson [n. 17]: 13-14.

25. Jolowicz [n. 17]: 34; Stern [n. 11] 1, pt. 2: 474.

26. E.g., E. Landshuth, *Toledoth 'Anshei Hashem Ufeulatham Baadath Berlin* [H] (Berlin 1884): 20-23; M. Freudenthal, *Aus der Heimat Mendelssohns* (Berlin 1900): 197; Horowitz [n. 7]: 21-22.

27. Freudenthal [n. 26]: 271-76; C. Roth, *History of the Great Synagogue* (London 1950): 71.

28. Meisl [n. 18]: 1-127; Jacobson [n. 17]: 25-76.

29. Stern [n. 11] 1, pt. 2: 474.

30. Ibid.: 408-9; 2, pt. 2: 14, 335; König [n. 17]: 230. This is implied since each immigrant teacher had to state he really was a *melamed* under oath.

31. *Festschrift zum 200 jährigen Bestehen des israelitischen Vereins für Krankenpflege und Beerdigung Chevra Kaddischa zu Königsberg i. Pr.* (Königsberg 1904): 6; Jolowicz [n. 17]: 34, 38 n. 1, 40, 54, 65-66; Stern [n. 11] 2, pt. 1: 163.

32. See above [n. 28]. See also Stern [n. 11] 2, pt. 2: 335.

33. M. Freudenthal, *Leipziger Messgäste* (Frankfort/Main 1928): 84; idem [n. 26]: 195; König [n. 17]: 256; Horowitz [n. 7]: 15; Shohet [n. 1]: 178, 181; S. J. Finn, *Qiryah Ne'emanah* [H] (Vilna 1915): 107; P. Philippson, *Biographische Skizzen* 1-2 (Leipzig 1864): 19 (family from Cracow lived in Arnswalde, Neumark). See also Stern [n. 11] 2, pt. 2: 95, 178-79, 232, 330, 503, 718, 728, 763, 793-94; Shohet [n. 1]: 179.

34. Koeltzsch [n. 21]: 10, 39-40; E. Lehmann, *Der polnische Resident Berend Lehmann* (Dresden 1885): 66.

35. E. Shulman, *Sefath Yehudith-Ashkenazith Vesifruthah* [H] (Riga 1913): 168; Freudenthal [n. 33]: 131; S. Goldschmidt, *Geschichte der Beerdigungsbruderschaft . . . in Hamburg* (Hamburg 1912): 22-24; M. Hagiz, *Mishnath Ḥakhamim*: 15a, quoted by

Shohet [n. 1]: 270 n. 36; A. Rexhausen, *Die rechtliche und
wirtschaftliche Lage der Juden im Hochstift Hildesheim* (Hildesheim 1914): 130, 151-57; MGDJ 1 (1909): 122; M.
Zucker-
mann, *Dokumente zur Geschichte der Juden in Hannover* (Hanover 1908): 43; S. Carlebach, *Geschichte der Juden in Lübeck
und Moisling* (Lübeck 1898): 27; JJGSH 8 (1936-37): 91; BJGL
3 (1901): 150.

36. Hallo [n. 22]: 90; Landshuth [n. 26]: 37; D. Kaufmann, *Aus
Heinrich Heine's Ahnensaal* (Breslau 1896): 284; Auerbach [n.
8]; Emden [n. 12]: 108; L. Löwenstein, *Geschichte der Juden in
der Kurpfalz* (Frankfort/Main 1895): 138, 198, 224; Shohet [n.
1]: 184, 298 n. 106; C. Duschinsky, *Gedenkbücher von Offenbach a. Main* (Frankfort/Main 1924): 20-31; Barbeck [n. 16]: 57;
BJGL 1 (1899): 36; 3 (1901): 56, 132-33, 154-57.

37. Dr. jur. Victor [n. 23]; D. Simonsen in *Jüdische Presse* (Sabat
Stunde sect.) 26 (1895): 20; Carlebach [n. 35]: 33.

38. *Yivo Bleter* [Y] 36 (1952): 25; intro., Shabethai Cohen's *Gevu-
rath 'Anashim* [H] (Dessau 1697); Gold [n. 20]: 114, 185, 269,
297.

39. For Vienna's Jewish community, see M. Grunwald, *Vienna*
(Philadelphia 1936): 123-29, 135-38; for immigrants from Poland, see B. Wachstein, *Die Inschriften des alten Judenfriedhofs
in Wien* 1 (Vienna 1912): 58, 163; 2: 69, 119, 145, 275, 283,
406; also cf. Moses Lvov's approbation to *Heshiv Rabbi 'Eli'ezer.*

40. Berndt [n. 20]: 35; according to a Silesian ordinance of 18 Dec.
1737, "a large number" of Polish Jews "sneaked in" (42).

41. *Kelilath Yofi* 2: 32b, 33a; Freudenthal [n. 26]: 195. It is possible
Silesian ordinance [n. 40] refers to *Betteljuden,* who were then
very numerous. Cf. Berndt [n. 20] (Jewish population of Glogau
became very large), who is obviously of opinion increase resulted
from illegal immigration of Jews from Poland.

42. PAJHS 48 (1958-59): 21-22; *Pene Yehoshu'a* [H] (Lemberg
1860), intro.; *Haẓofeh* 4 (1915): 287; *Yivo Bleter* 17 (1941):
148; Horowitz [n. 7]: 8-9, 21-22; Meisels [n. 10].

43. *Ya'aroth Devash* [H] (Jozefow 1865): 133; Z. Szajkowski in
Yivo Bleter 39 (1955): 83; S. Posener in JSS 7 (1945): 214.

44. M. H. Stern, *Americans of Jewish Descent* (Cincinnati 1960):
2, 87; TJHSE 5 (1908): 150, 153; Roth [n. 27]: 81, 83; B. Shill-
man, *A Short History of the Jews in Ireland* (Dublin 1945): 46;
MJHSE 6 (1962): 184-85 (London), 192 (Plymouth).

45. Isaac Pollack, who lived in New York and Newport c. 1737, may
have been native of Holland or England (PAJHS 48 [1958]: 18).
Immigrants from Lithuania by way of Holland were 2 brothers
from Zager living in Dutch Surinam. A list of wills before 1800

of Jews of Barbados, Jamaica, and British Guiana, contains no names indicating Eastern European origin (S. Oppenheim in PAJHS 32 [1931]: 55-64).

46. *Ḥiburei Liqutim* [n. 2]: 3a; C. Roth, *The Rise of Provincial Jewry* (London 1950): 93; idem [n. 27]: 82; Stern [n. 44]: 2, 64; Freudenthal [n. 26]: 299; BJGL 3 (1901): 38-39.

47. Cf., e.g., Shohet [n. 1]: 181; Rexhausen [n. 35]: 151-57. Of course, most yeshivah students who went to Germany were young men. See also MJHSE 6 (1962): 192.

48. Emden [n. 12]: 124-26. Quotation is from work by missionary J. P. Callenberg (see Shohet [n. 1]: 319 n. 107a).

49. Asaf [n. 12]: 123; Hallo [n. 22]; JFF 2 (1925-26): 142-43; Emden [n. 12]: 125. For *melamdim* my sample list of emigrants' occupations does not confirm picture obtained from literary sources, but it is possible many teachers appear in them as "rabbis."

50. M. Hagiz, *Mishnath Ḥakhamim*: 15a, quoted by Shohet [n. 1]: 279 n. 36. It is doubtful that most resident scholars in German *Klausen* were from Poland, as stated by Shohet (90). At least this was not so in Behrend Lehman's *Klaus* in Halberstadt; according to authority quoted by Shohet (Auerbach [n. 8]: 62), only one scholar there was from Poland. See also Finn [n. 33]: 109; *Ḥiburei Liqutim* [n. 2], intro. For Italy, see my *Jewish Life in Renaissance Italy* [H] (New York 1955): 140ff.

51. Jacobson [n. 17]: 36, 50-51, 94-113; Meisl [n. 18]; Freudenthal [n. 33] *pass.*; Stern [n. 11] 2, pt. 1: 163; pt. 2: 96, 330. MGJV 22 (1907): 46-47; BJGL 3 (1901): 150, 154-55.

52. H. I. Bloom, *The Economic Activities of the Jews of Amsterdam in the Seventeenth and Eighteenth Centuries* (Williamsport, Pa., 1937): 210 ff.; PAJHS 48 (1958-59): 21-22.

53. Jacobson [n. 17]: 91; Shohet [n. 1]: 181, 185. Cf. also lists of proofreaders in Freudenthal [n. 26]: 271-76.

54. Haenle [n. 16]: 136; L. Müller, "Aus fünf Jahrhunderten: Beiträge zur Geschichte der jüdischen Gemeinden im Riess," *Zeitschrift des Historischen Vereins für Schwaben und Neuburg* 26 (1899): 113; H. Bodemeyer, *Die Juden: Ein Beitrag zur Hannoverschen Rechtsgeschichte* (Göttingen 1855): 18; Stern [n. 11] 2, pt. 2: 350; *Ya'aroth Devash*: 133. Description is modeled on Lam. 1:6 and Deut. 8:4. For why we must assume majority of *Betteljuden* were Polish, see above [intro. n. 15].

55. König [n. 17]: 228; a Prussian ordinance (*Erneuertes und geschärftes Edict wegen der überhandnehmenden fremden Bettel-Juden* [Berlin 12 Dec. 1780]) cites 7 other decrees against *Betteljuden*, 1719-49; I. Freund, *Die Emanzipation der Juden in Preussen* 2 (Berlin 1912): 43-44; Stern [n. 11] 2, pt. 2: 82, 352,

463; Bodemeyer [n. 54]; A. Loeb, *Die Rechtsverhältnisse der Juden im . . . Königreiche . . . Hannover* (Frankfort/Main 1908): 16.

56. Barbeck [n. 16]: 71; C. T. Weiss, *Geschichte der Juden und rechtliche Stellung der Juden im Fürstbistum Strassburg, besonders in dem jetzt badischen Teile, nach Akten dargestellt* (Bonn 1896): 59; G. Anklam, *Die Judengemeinde Aurich* (Frankfort/Main 1927): 9.

57. Koeltzsch [n. 21]: 203 ff. Text of duke of Ansbach's instructions to his ambassador in Regensburg is in Stern [n. 11] 2, pt. 2: 350.

58. Emden [n. 12]: 107; Liebe [n. 17]: 104; Freund [n. 55]; Stern [n. 11] 2, pt. 1: 87; pt. 2: 97, 530; König [n. 17]: 228; Barbeck [n. 16]: 58.

59. Text of poem on Frankfort/Main is in *Yivo Studies in Philology* 2 (1928): 169 ff. See also Koeltzsch [n. 21]: 302; Haenle [n. 16]: 91; Anklam [n. 56]; Müller [n. 54]; Barbeck [n. 16]: 58; Stern [n. 11] 2, pt. 2: 351.

60. Zion n.s. 9 (1944): 33. In all, 4 families of immigrants in small town of Treuenbrietzen had 16 children (Stern [n. 11] 2, pt. 2: 178-79). In 1706, 3 immigrant families in Königsberg had 3, 4, and 5 children (see Jolowicz [n. 17]: 34); of course, some or all of them may have been born after their parents came west.

61. Shohet [n. 1]: 18.

62. Stern [n. 11] 2, pt. 2: 178-79. None of these families bore names indicating Polish origin. Of many lists in Stern of Jewish inhabitants in various Prussian cities, this is only one giving places of origin.

63. Ibid. 1, pt. 2: 468-72; 2, pt. 1: 163; pt. 2: 95, 335, 375, 721; Jolowicz [n. 17]: 34, 88; Meisl [n. 27]; Jacobson [n. 17]: 25-76.

64. Dr. jur. Victor [n. 23]; Shohet [n. 1]: 270; Carlebach [n. 35]: 33; Rexhausen [n. 35]: 151-57. However, cf. BJGL (3 [1901]: 114-19, 150-52, 170-71): immigrants were 8% of Jewish population in Hildesheim.

65. Z. H. Edelmann, *Gedulath Sha'ul* [H] (London 1852): 34a (Holleschau); Wachstein [n. 39] 2: 123 (Eibenschütz).

66. Statistics re Amsterdam's Jewry are in Bloom [n. 52]: 32, 210. Cf. above, however [ch. 2 n. 93].

67. König [n. 17]: 233; Freund [n. 55]; Koeltzsch [n. 21]: 302; Haenle [n. 16]: 134; Müller [n. 54]; Roth [n. 27]. However, due to expulsion from Prague, number of Bohemian *Betteljuden* increased considerably c. 1740-50. Cf. *Zion* 28 (1963): 158 n. 151.

68. Meisl [n. 18].

69. *Festschrift* [n. 31]: 20; J. Taglicht, *Nachlässe der Wiener Juden* (Vienna 1917): 288; C. Duschinsky, *Gedenkbücher (Memorbücher) von Offenbach a. Main u. anderen deutschen Gemeinden*

(Frankfort/Main 1924): 27-38; Stern [n. 44]: 2. Immigrants who obtained *Schutzbriefe* are mentioned in many sources cited in this ch.; e.g. Rexhausen [n. 35]: 130, 158-59; *Festschrift* [n. 31]: 20 n. 2.

70. Emden [n. 12]: 125, 177.
71. Rexhausen [n. 35]: 151-57; Landshuth [n. 26]: 20-23; JJLG 8 (1910): 119-20; *Kelilath Yofi* 2: 67b-69b; Edelmann [n. 65]; Jacobson [n. 17], *pass.*; Wachstein [n. 39]: 275.
72. *Ḥiburei Liqutim* [n. 2], intro.; Meisl [n. 18]; Freudenthal [n. 33], *pass.*; Jolowicz [n. 17]: 66; Stern [n. 11] 2, pt. 1: 105; *Festschrift* [n. 31]: 20 n. 2; Landshuth [n. 26]; PAJHS 48 (1958): 19-27; MJHSE 6 (1962): 143-74.
73. PAJHS, ibid.; Philippson [n. 33]; Freudenthal [n. 33].
74. Shohet [n. 1]: 306 n. 73; ZGJD 2 (1888): 95; *Gedenkboek . . . Jongenweeshuis* "Megadlé Jethomim" te Amsterdam (Amsterdam 1938): 117; Wachstein [n. 39] 2: 458; *Festschrift* [n. 31]: 32; Meisl [n. 18]. Of course, it is possible philanthropists named Polack were not immigrants but their sons.
75. *Festschrift* [n. 31]: 20; Landshuth [n. 26]: 20-23, 25, 37; Roth [n. 27]: 83; MGWJ 42 (1898): 134; Horowitz [n. 7]: 21-22; *Sefunoth* [H] 9 (1964): 215 (in 1710 Aron Abrahams Pollack was a *parnas* of Ashkenazic community in Amsterdam). Meisl [n. 18]. M. Grunwald, *Hamburgs deutsche Juden* (Hamburg 1904): 19, 39, 40.
76. Landshuth [n. 26]; Auerbach [n. 8]: 64-68; JJLG 8 (1910): 119-21; 6 (1908): 177-86; Z. H. Berlin, *Zava Rav* [H], ed. Z. Y. Michelson (Piotrkow 1908), intro.; Horowitz [n. 7]: 76 n. 3; EJ 6: 304-14; Shohet [n. 1]: 175. For descendants of Rabbi Baruch Kahana (Rappaport), their intermarriages, and rabbinic posts, see BJGL 1 (1900): 22-23, 36-37.

CHAPTER FOUR

1. See S. M. Dubnow, *History of the Jews in Russia and Poland* 1 (Philadelphia 1916): 180-87, 262-97, esp. 266 (passage from a nobleman's diary).
2. Z. Horowitz, *Kithvei Hage'onim* [H] (New York 1959): 81-82; C. Roth in MJHSE 3 (1937): 2-3; L. Donath, *Geschichte der Juden in Mecklenburg* (Leipzig 1874): 153 n. 138; A. Kober, *Cologne* (Philadelphia 1940): 370; *Hafla'ah* [H] (Lemberg 1816), intro.; C. Roth, *A History of the Jews in England* (Oxford 1941): 234; TJHSE 17 (1953): 92.

3. J. Klausner, *Historyah shel hasifruth ha'ivrith haḥadashah* [H] 1 (Jerusalem 1930): 156-58; *Yivo Studies in Philology* 3 (1929): 539, 552.

4. S. Maimon, *An Autobiography* (New York 1947): 68, MGWJ 14 (1865): 261; I. Euchel, *Toledoth . . . Mosheh ben Menaḥem* [H] (Berlin 1789): 10b; I. Samosch, *'Aruboth Ḥashamayim,* intro., quoted in B. Katz, *Rabanuth, Ḥasiduth, Haskalah* 1 (Tel Aviv 1956): 143; S. Bennett, *The Present Reign of the Synagogue of Duke's Place* (London 1818): 2; H. Wessely, *Divrei Shalom We'emeth* [H], 2d ed. (Vienna 1826): 45; Donath [n. 2]: 319-20.

5. Horowitz [n. 2]: 81-82, 137; E. Katzenellenbogen, *Zekher Zaddiq* [H] (Altona 1805), sect. "Ma'allei 'Ish": 10b; Maimon [n. 4]: 72, 101-2.

6. S. Löwenstamm, *Binyan 'Ariel* [H] (Amsterdam 1778), intro.; JJLG 19 (1928): 55. Great need for Polish teachers in southern Germany also is evident from J. Isaak, *Gedanken über Betteljuden* (Nuremberg 1791): 43. *Ketav Yosher* quotation is from Katz [n. 4]: 241. See also JJLG 8 (1910), H. sect.: 91 ff. Since Moses Wasserzug was born c. 1750, it may be assumed his trip to Frankfort/Oder was c. 1770-75. That Germany was destination of Polish Jews desiring to escape their troubles is evident in comedy *Als der Sof iz Gout iz Alles* Gout (ed. L. Fuks [Paris 1955]), which no doubt describes situation in Germany rather than Holland (7, 9). E. Shulman *(Sefath Yehudith-Ashkenazith Vesifruthah* [H] [Riga 1913]: 168) describes a poem of 1675 whose theme is almost identical with comedy's.

7. JSS (1945): 200; J. Jacobson, *Die Judenbürgerbücher der Stadt Berlin* (Berlin 1962): 3; F. Priebatsch in *Festschrift Dietrich Schäfer* (Jena 1916): 617; A. Löb, *Die . . . Juden im Königreiche . . . Hannover* (Frankfort/Main 1908): 18; M. Balaban, *Dzieje Żydów w Galicji* (Lemberg n.d.): 27-28.

8. Frederick the Great's policy toward his many new Jewish subjects in West Prussia is described in detail by L. Comber in *Bleter far geszichte* [Y] 1 (1934): 75-85, esp. 77. See also H. Gregoire, *An Essay on the Physical, Moral and Political Reformation of the Jews* (London n.d.): 77-78; Maimon [n. 4]: 72-74; *Erneuertes und geschärftes Edict wegen der Überhandnehmenden fremden Bettel-Juden* (Berlin 12 Dec. 1780); M. Brann, *Geschichte der Gesellschaft der Brüder* (Breslau 1880): 9; C. W. Dohm, *Über die bürgerliche Verbesserung der Juden* 2 (Berlin 1783): 290-92.

9. *Zeitschrift für vaterländische Geschichte und Altertumskunde* 61 (1903): 206-7; S. Haenle, *Geschichte der Juden im ehemaligen Fürstenthum Ansbach* (Ansbach 1867): 102; Donath [n. 2]: 319-21.

10. JSS 5 (1943): 177-78; C. Roth, *History of the Great Synagogue* (London 1950): 202; J. Grätzer, *Geschichte der israelitischen Kranken-Verpflägungsanstalt . . . zu Breslau* (Breslau 1841): 41; S. Posener in JSS 1 (1939): 291; Z. H. Ilfeld, *Divrei Negidim* [H] (Amsterdam 1799): 20b. Cf. H. I. Bloom, "Felix Libertate and the Emancipation of Dutch Jewry," in *Essays on Jewish Life and Thought* (New York 1959): 105-22.

11. Posener [n. 10] obviously overlooks *Betteljuden* problem when he attempts to prove these statements were exaggerated as far as France is concerned.

12. JFF 2 (1925-26): 119-71.

13. *Festschrift zum 200 jährigen Bestehen des israelitischen Vereins für Krankenpflege und Beerdigung Chevra Kaddischa zu Königsberg i. Pr.* (Königsberg 1904): 1-38; Jacobson [n. 7]: 51-92; Maimon [n. 4]: 56; H. Greenstein, *The Rise of the Jewish Community of New York* (Philadelphia 1947): 22. For emigrants from Flatow (Zlotowo), cf. *Königsberg Festschrift*: 6, 16, 21, 25; JFF 2: 147. For emigrants from Zamość and reasons for emigration, cf. J. Shatzky in *Yivo Bleter* 36 (1952): 24-39. See also C. Reznikoff and U. Z. Engelman, *The Jews of Charleston* (Philadelphia 1950): 91; JFF 2: 170.

14. J. Picciotto, *Sketches of Anglo-Jewish History* (London 1956): 171; Roth [n. 2]: 233-34. List of 36 immigrant families living in Mecklenburg-Schwerin in 1769 contains none from the Ukraine; one would expect some Ukrainian Jews should be found there a year after slaughter of Uman. Riots usually did not start large scale emigration (see above [intro. nn. 21-22, 24]). See also I. Schipper in *Neue Jüdische Monatshefte* 2 (1917-18): 229 (his number of emigrants from Galicia seems to be very much exaggerated).

15. TJHSE [n. 2]; Kober [2]: 369; Picciotto [n. 14]: 171, 465 n. 3; Maimon [n. 4]: 57.

16. E. M. Dreifuss, *Die Familiennamen der Juden* (Frankfort/Main 1927).

17. *Sippurim* [H] 3, ed. W. Pascheles (Prague 1854): 151. Jost's recollections are of 1803; there is no doubt, however, situation was no different before 1800.

18. Jacobson [n. 7]: 51-92; only a fraction of Berlin's Jewry was admitted to citizenship then (1809).

19. JJLG 19 (1928): 45; 8 (1910), H sect.: 92, 94; E. Landshuth, *Toledoth 'Anshei Hashem Ufeulatham Baadath Berlin* [H] (Berlin 1884): 33, 75; MZJV n.s. 1 (1905): 96; M. Freudenthal, *Aus der Heimat Mendelssohns* (Berlin 1900): 138; M. Köhler, *Die Juden in Halberstadt und Umgebung bis zur Emanzipation* (Berlin 1927): 13; *Festschrift* [n. 13]: 1-39 (of 255 Jews who

died there, 1770-1810, 105 were from Poland; however, some were not immigrants but patients seeking medical help). For Breslau, see Brann [n. 8]: 9, 11-12; Horowitz [n. 2]: 48, 65; F. Bloch, *Die Juden in Militsch* (Breslau 1926): 19; Grätzer [n. 10].

20. My list of immigrants to Germany shows few settled in Saxony. A Berlin banker, native of Posen, later settled in Dresden. Marcus Jost's father, native of Jaroslaw, became a *Schutzjude* in duchy of Anhalt (1780). See Pascheles [n. 17]: 145.

21. *Festskrift I Anledning Af Professor David Simonsens 70 Aarige Fodselsdag* (Copenhagen 1923): 353 (Hamburg); S. Gronemann, *Genealogische Studien über die alten jüdischen Familien Hannovers* (Berlin 1913): 69-71, 124, (H sect.) 51-54, 111, 145 (Hanover); ibid.: 108 (Emden, Hildesheim); JFF [n. 12]; Donath [n. 2]: 323 (Mecklenburg). Two places where bans allegedly forbid Jewish resettlement, Spain and duchy of Mecklenburg, expelled Jews in same year (1492)!

22. S. Carlebach, *Geschichte der Juden in Lübeck und Moisling* (Lübeck 1898): 33; M. Stern, *Die jüdische Bevölkerung der deutschen Städte* 2 (Kiel 1892): 42; Gronemann [n. 21]: 60; M. Rosenmann, *Isak Noa Mannheimer* (Vienna 1922): 24; *Yearbook of the Leo Baeck Institute* 3 (1958): 317; A. Human, *Geschichte der Juden in Sachsen-Meiningen-Hildburghausen*, 2d ed. (Weimar 1939): 142; M. Balaban, *Letoledoth Hatenu'ah Hafranqith* [H] 1 (Tel Aviv 1934): 295.

23. For Frankfort/Main, see Aron of Copenhagen, *'Or Hayashar* [H] (Amsterdam 1769): 85a; I. Lipschitz, *'Or Israel* [H] (Cleves 1770): 112b; A. Schiff, *Die Namen der Frankfurter Juden* (Freiburg/B. 1917): 40, 42; Horowitz [n. 2]: 67-68, 137; *Sefer Hayovel Huval Shay Likhevod Nahum Sokolow* [H] (Warsaw 1904): 456; Shatzky [n. 13]: 29. See also *'Or Hayashar*: 82a (Cologne); Kober [n. 2]; C. Duschinsky, *Gedenkbücher (Memorbücher) von Offenbach a. Main u. anderen deutschen Gemeinden* (Frankfort/Main 1924): 40-75 (not always, however, can we be sure a given immigrant had not lived in Offenbach before 1750); JSS 5 (1943): 178 (Paderborn); JJLG 14 (1922): 22-24 (Hanau); C. Roth, *The Rise of Provincial Jewry* (London 1950): 93 n. (Düsseldorf); S. Salfeld, *Bilder aus der Vergangenheit der jüdischen Gemeinde Mainz* (Mayence 1903): 74; S. Samuel, *Geschichte der Juden in Stadt und Stift Essen* (Essen 1905): 77; JFF [n. 12]: 130 (Bonn). For Frankists in Offenbach, see A. Kraushaar, *Frank i Frankiści Polscy* 2 (Cracow 1895): 154. See also G. Scholem in *Beth Israel Bepolin* [H] 2 (Jerusalem 1953): 75 n. 46.

24. Dreifuss [n. 16]: 51, 54, 72 (Samst [Zamość], Pommer, Bolack, Staschower).

25. Maimon [n. 4]: 65-68; JJLG 6 (1908): 199-202; M. Weinberg, *Die Memorbücher der jüdischen Gemeinden in Bayern* (Frankfort/Main 1937): 71; idem, *Geschichte der Juden in der Oberpfalz* 3 (Sulzbürg 1909): 171.

26. B. Friedberg, *Geschichte der Familie Horowitz* (Antwerp 1928): 2-18; H. Gold, *Die Juden . . . Mährens . . .* (Brünn 1929): 174, 297, 556, 573, 582; A. Frankl-Gruen, *Geschichte der Juden in Kremsier* 1 (Breslau 1896): 81-85.

27. G. Wolf, *Die jüdischen Friedhöfe* (Vienna 1879): 21; J. Taglicht, *Nachlässe der Wiener Juden* (Vienna 1917): 198, 201, 237; B. Wachstein, *Inschriften . . . Wien* 2 (Vienna 1912): 401, 411; 487 (Innsbruck). See M. Grunwald (*Vienna* [Philadelphia 1936]: 184-87) for how Jews managed to stay there illegally. For Polish Jews in Viennese cartoon, see A. Rubens, *A Jewish Iconography* (London 1954): 60.

28. *Hazofeh* [H] 8 (1924): 299; C. J. D. Asulai, *Maʿgal Tōb Ha-Salem* [H] (Jerusalem 1934): 133; H. I. Bloom, *The Economic Activities of the Jews of Amsterdam in the Seventeenth and Eighteenth Centuries* (Williamsport, Pa., 1937): 110; *Yivo Bleter* 10 (1936): 110, 236; Horowitz [n. 2]: 10; J. Zwarts, *Gedenkschrift bij het tweede eeuwfeest der Synagoge te Amersfoort* (Amersfoort 1927): 52; *'Or Hayashar* [n. 23]: 21b. Many people named Pollack lived in Holland (e.g., Groningen [see JFF 14 (1938): 903-4]), but it is hard to determine whether they were immigrants or their descendants. According to legend current among Jews in Holland, Gaon of Vilna stayed a short time in Oldenzaal (near German border) on his peregrinations. Cf. *Reshumoth* [H] n.s. 1 (1946): 126 n. 3.

29. Human [n. 22]; *Hazofeh* 8 (1924): 292; Ilfeld [n. 10] (speech of deputy van Hamelsveld, 22 Aug. 1796).

30. Z. Hurwitz lived in Metz before settling in Paris (see EJ 8: 292). See also JSS 1 (1939): 292; 6 (1944): 38; 7 (1945): 222-23; M. Ginsburger, *Der israelitische Friedhof in Jungholz* (Gebweiler 1904): 119-27.

31. TJHSE 19 (1960): 17; *Hazofeh* 4 (1914): 3; Roth [n. 10]: 71 97, 191, 202; TJHSE 17 (1953): 253; MJHSE 6 (1962): 190-91; A. Levy, *History of the Sunderland Jewish Community* (London 1956): 30, 35, 36. When proselyte Lord George Gordon was in jail, he was assisted at Saturday services by *minyan* composed entirely of Polish Jews (see TJHSE 20 [1964]: 78). JQR n.s. 10 (1919-20): 459; TJHSE 5 (1908): 150; Roth [n. 23]: 54, 62.

32. J. R. Rosenbloom, *A Biographical Dictionary of Early American Jews* (Louisville 1960); J. R. Marcus, *Early American Jewry* 1 (Philadelphia 1951): 89, 153; 2 (1953): 68, 276, 339; M. H. Stern, *Americans of Jewish Descent* (Cincinnati 1960): 2, 4,

29, 64, 83, 87, 89, 120, 181, 185; E. Wolf and M. Whiteman, *The History of the Jews of Philadelphia* (Philadelphia 1957): 31, 123, 418; Reznikoff [n. 13]: 50; J. R. Marcus, *American Jewry Documents: Eighteenth Century* (Cincinnati 1959): 172, 451; I. Rivkind in PAJHS 34 (1937): 70-72.

33. For Polish Jewish immigrants to America from England and Ireland, see Stern [n. 32]: 24, 87, 89; Polish immigrants to England from Germany, e.g., in Roth [n. 10]: 159 n. 9, 194-95; idem [n. 23]; JFF [n. 12]: 146; EJ 6: 101-2; 8: 292; Klausner [n. 3]. See also E. Duckesz, *Iwoh Lemoschaw* [H] (Cracow 1903): 59.

34. Jacobson [n. 7]: 58-95; MJHSE [n. 31].

35. A. Barnett, *The Western Synagogue Through Two Centuries* (London 1961): 51.

36. Carlebach [n. 22]; Katzenellenbogen [n. 5]; S. Bennett, "Introduction to the Consistency of Israel," Ger. tr. S. Kirschstein in *Jüdische Graphiker* (Berlin 1918): 16-19.

37. For other Polish rabbis of important western communities, see Duckesz [n. 33]: 53-59, 63-74, 77-83; Friedberg [n. 26]; Kober [n. 2]; Carlebach [n. 22]; Horowitz [n. 2]: 18.

38. JJLG 8 [n. 6]; Fuks [n. 6]: 29; Roth [n. 10]: 71, 87; *The Case and Appeal of James Ashley* (London 1753): 13; *Yivo Bleter* 17 (1941): 151; Weinberg [n. 25 (1)].

39. JSS [n. 23]; JFF [n. 12]; JJLG 19 (1928): 45 n. 1, 53; Wessely [n. 4]: 17.

40. See Katzenellenbogen [n. 5]: 11a-b (Raphael Cohn, rabbi of Hamburg, went to Germany to publ. a book). We may assume some of many authors and scholars Moses Körner (*Rishpei Qesheth* [Hanover 1831]) found all over Germany had arrived before 1800. See also *Yivo Bleter* 10 (1936): 234; JJLG 19 (1928): 54. There is no reason to question L. Joseph's veracity, though he was clearly hostile to alien authors.

41. TJHSE 5 (1908): 158; Maimon [n. 4], *pass.*

42. JFF [n. 12]; Gold [n. 26]: 256. A tailor from Poland migrated as far as America (see Reznikoff [n. 32]).

43. R. Mahler, *Yidn in Amoliqn Poyln in Likht fun Ziffern* [Y] (Warsaw 1958): 197.

44. JFF [n. 12]; Pascheles [n. 20]; Mahler [n. 43]: 113-14; MJHSE 6 (1962): 190-91.

45. M. Freudenthal, *Leipziger Messgäste* (Frankfort/Main 1928), *pass.*, esp.: 15.

46. Stern [n. 32]: 29; Marcus [n. 32 (1)] 2: 68; Wolf [n. 32]: 418; Marcus [n. 32 (2)]: 451; JFF [n. 12], esp.: 147; Z. H. Edelman, *Gedulath Sha'ul* [H] (London, 1852): 36b-37a.

47. S. Pfeifer (*Kulturgeschichtliche Bilder aus Reckendorf* [Bamberg n.d.]: 74) (most wandering Jews were natives of Bavaria and other areas in Germany). City council of Lixheim in Lorraine stated in 1790 that "bands of German, Polish, Turkish, and other Jews" were arriving daily in "squadrons" (see Z. Szajkowski in HJ 21 [1959]: 24). Many wandering Jews in Franconia, whose fate is discussed by Isaak ([n. 6], esp.: 20, 25), also seem to have been local poor Jews.

48. HJ [n. 47]; Pfeifer [n. 47] (6 individual beggars and 2 with wives are described as "Pollaks"; one also had a child). See also B. H. Auerbach, *Geschichte der israelitischen Gemeinde Halberstadt* (Halberstadt 1866): 113, 119 ("jüdisch-polnische Landstreicher"); Human [n. 22]: 141-42; Löb [n. 7]; Z. Szajkowski, *Franco-Judaica* (New York 1962): 10.

49. For epistle of Gaon of Vilna, see *Mesilath Yesharim* [H] (Jerusalem n.d.): 72. Rigid laws against *Betteljuden* [see nn. 47-48] in Halberstadt provided for admission of pregnant women (see Köhler [n. 19]: 81). Among wanderers who invaded Isle-sur-Sorg in 1773 were several pregnant women (see JSS 7 [1945]: 222-23). See also Isaak [n. 6]: 20; Marcus [n. 32 (2)]: 172 ("two gentleman [*sic*] from Poland . . . requested [Philadelphia] congregation to afford them assistance").

50. Köhler [n. 19]: 79; J. G. Krünitz (*Oeconomische Encyclopädie* [Brünn 1789]: 501) is no doubt objective and accurate in his report of wandering Jews converging on Berlin. Isaak [n. 6]: 17.

51. Maimon [n. 4]: 63; Fuks [n. 6]: Isaak [n. 6]: 9, 25; A. F. Thiele, *Die jüdischen Gauner in Deutschland* (Berlin 1841): 11-12; Picciotto [n. 15].

52. Official appointed by community of Halberstadt to supervise wandering Jews was instructed to search for them in various inns "every day." See Köhler [n. 19]: 91-93; Krünitz [n. 50]; Isaak [n. 6]: 14; Haenle [n. 9]: 133.

53. Cf. *Edict* [n. 8]. Krünitz says "eine Menge" (multitude) of *Betteljuden* arrived for holidays in Berlin [n. 50].

54. Human [n. 48]; Donath [n. 2]: 321; *Yearbook* [n. 22]; Carlebach [n. 22]: 30 n. 2; H. Bodemeyer, *Die Juden: Ein Beitrag zur Hannoverschen Rechtgeschichte* (Göttingen 1855): 19; Löb [n. 7].

55. ZGJD n.s. 6 (1935): 230; Isaak [n. 6]: 11-12, 20.

56. JSS 7 (1945): 222-24; HJ [n. 47].

57. Roth [n. 10]: 191 n. 3.

58. *Edict* [n. 8]; Isaak [n. 6]: 6; Maimon [n. 4]: 62; Köhler [n. 52]; Roth [n. 2]: 233-34.

59. I. Seligmann ben Abraham, *Minḥath 'Ani Uminḥath Kohen*

[H] Amsterdam (1769): 6a (his use of *'orehim* is to be understood as in Yiddish, i.e., poor people, homeless wanderers). A. Shohet (*Beginnings of the Haskalah Among German Jewry* [Jerusalem 1960]: 281 n. 24) erroneously says this happened when Levi Saul (Aryeh Löb) Löwenstamm was rabbi in Amsterdam.

60. Köhler [n. 52]; Isaak [n. 6]: 9, 10, 15, 16; JSS [n. 56]; Weinberg [n. 25 (2)]: 166 .
61. Isaak [n. 6], esp.: 5, 28, 36; ZGJD [n. 55]; Haenle [n. 9]: 138.
62. Mahler ([n. 43]: 184) proves average Jewish family in Poland had 5 or 6 members in 1764.
63. Ibid.: 45.
64. J. Meisl, ed., *Protokollbuch der jüdischen Gemeinde Berlin (1723-1854)* (Jerusalem 1962): 152-401; Jacobson [n. 7]: 51-95.
65. JJLG 19 (1928): 43-44, 53; Brann [n. 8]: 11-12.
66. Brann, ibid.
67. *Festschrift* [n. 13], *pass.*; H. Jolowicz, *Geschichte der Juden in Königsberg* (Posen 1867): 88. For a Polish scholar-patient in Königsberg, see intro. to Zvi ben Samuel's *Margalioth Hatorah* [H] (Poryck 1788). See A. Yaari, *Mehqerei Sefer* [H] (Jerusalem 1958): 112.
68. *Bützowsche Nebenstunden* 6 (1769), rpt. JFF [n. 12].
69. Of 18 *melamdim* who taught in Bützow, 1738-69, 17 were from Poland [n. 68]. To be sure, some may in fact have had other occupations and registered as *melamdim* only to gain residence rights.
70. Dreifuss [n. 16]: 97.
71. Maimon [n. 4]: 65-68.
72. Jacobson ([n. 7]: 17) disputes H. Graetz' view (*Geschichte der Juden,* 2d ed. [Leipzig n.d.] 2: 599-601) of size of conversion movement among German Jews at turn of cent., but admits it was *nicht unerheblich* (considerable).
73. Shohet [n. 59]: 18-19.
74. S. M. Dubnow, *Weltgeschichte des jüdischen Volkes* 8 (Berlin 1928): 16.
75. Bloom [n. 28]: 31-32. It is estimated c. 50,000 Jews then lived in Holland. Cf. Bloom [n. 10]: 119.
76. JSS 1 (1939): 291.
77. V. D. Lipman, ed., *Three Centuries of Anglo-Jewish History* (Cambridge 1961): 61; Roth [n. 2]: 233; MJHSE 3 (1937): 5-6; Levy [n. 31]: 35-36.
78. E.g., Rosenbloom [n. 32]. One Polish family had 12 members (PAJHS 50 [1960]: 37, 41). To be sure, 1790 census lists only 4 Jewish families from Poland (ibid.: 46, 55, 64); however, early censuses are inaccurate and incomplete. Cf. AJHQ 53 (1964): 342.

79. *Edict* [n. 8]; Isaak [n. 6]: 15; ZGJD [n. 55]; Pascheles [n. 17].
80. Isaak [n. 6]: 16-17.
81. Ibid.
82. JSS 7 (1945): 222-23; 8 (1946): 182; HJ 21 (1959): 24. Of course *Betteljuden* in France came from Germany, but this need not influence our calculations of their number in Germany, because new wanderers were constantly coming from Poland. In addition, Isaak makes it clear that groups of *Betteljuden* were perpetually wandering back and forth between towns and cities. Germany, France, and other West European countries thus had "permanent" *Betteljuden* populations and our calculations for various localities apply solely to wanderers living in them.
83. In 1779 squadrons were 80-100 men (*Encyclopaedia Britannica*).
84. Ilfeld [n. 10]: 18a; Roth [n. 58].
85. Cf. Duckesz [n. 33]: 59, 72; Gronemann [n. 21]: 69-71, (H sect.) 108. See Kober [n. 2] for a re-immigrant (Rabbi Shraga Hellman) who returned to the West because of conditions in Poland; his migratory "career" was almost identical with Tobias the Physician's a century earlier.
86. Katzenellenbogen [n. 5]: 11a; Maimon [n. 4], esp.: 101-2.
87. *Hazofeh* 4 (1914): 5 (3 Pollacks); Ashley [n. 38] (the Polak); Fuks [n. 6]: 19 (Poleck). Nickname Pollack was still used recently in Holland to denote newcomers from Poland. Cf. *Reshumoth* [H] n.s. 1 (1946): 127.
88. J. Jacobson, *Jüdische Trauungen in Berlin 1723-1759* (Berlin 1938); idem [n. 7], *pass.*; JJLG 6 (1908): 199-202; Katzenellenbogen [n. 5]: 15b; Duschinsky [n. 23]: 63; JFF [n. 12]: 168-71. To be sure, there is no way to ascertain whether all women married by immigrants were natives.
89. JJLG [n. 23].
90. JJLG 6 (1908): 203-7; JFF 2 (1928-30): 147; D. Kaufmann and M. Freudenthal, *Die Familie Gomperz* (Frankfort/Main 1907): 74; Roth [n. 10]: 195.
91. Brann [n. 8]; *Hazofeh* [n. 29]; MJHSE 3 (1937): 2-6; Levy [n. 31]: 30, 36.
92. *Hazofeh* [n. 30]; TJHSE 19 (1960): 17; Mahler, *Divrei Yemei Yisra'el* [H] 1 (Merhavyah 1952): 214; Jacobson [n. 64] (Berlin); MJHSE 6 (1962): 190-94 (Plymouth); Rosenbloom [n. 32].
93. Fuks [n. 6]: 7.
94. Bennett [n. 4]: 4.
95. D. Kaufmann, *Aus Heinrich Heine's Ahnensaal* (Breslau 1896): 296; JSS 5 (1943): 177. Anecdote (Auerbach [n. 48]: 222-23) is in letter to Israel Jacobson, president of consistory of Jews of Westphalia, from S. Baruch, president of community in Bonn.

96. Fuks [n. 6], esp.: 6-9.
97. A portrait of Moses Samuel is repro. in Roth [n. 10], fac.: 194; of Solomon Bennett, in Barnett [n. 35], fac.: 51; of Mordecai M. Cohen, in Reznikoff [n. 13], fac.: 92. Katzenellenbogen [n. 5]: 15a; EJ 10: 586-90 (Ezekiel Landau); *Yivo Bleter* 36 (1952): 24; Wessely [n. 4]. On works by Maimon, see S. Atlas, "Solomon Maimon: The Man and his Thought," HJ 13 (1951): 109-20. See also, e.g., Bennett's pamphlet [n. 4]. EJ 6: 915-16 (Issachar Baer Falkensohn); 8: 140 (Judah Littvack), 292 (Zalkind Hurwitz). On Hyman Hurwitz, cf. C. Roth, *Magna Bibliotheca Anglo-Judaica* (London 1937); Marcus [n. 32 (1)] 2: 549.
98. Reznikoff [n. 13]: x; Jacobson [n. 64].
99. EJ 8: 292. For further info. on Z. Hurwitz and excerpts from his writings, see A. Z. Aescoly, *Ha'emansipazyah Hayehudith* [H] (Jerusalem 1952): 13 ff., 97-98.
100. JE 8: 140; EJ 10: 1059; Bloom [n. 28]: 218 n. 53. See also idem [n. 10]; J. Shatzky in *Yivo Bleter* [n. 40].
101. For activities of Polish *maskilim* in the West, see Klausner [n. 3]: 155-66, 244-57; Wessely [n. 4].
102. *Yivo Bleter* 10 (1936): 236; *Voice of Jacob* 3 (London 1844): 196; Rosenmann [n. 22].
103. M. Horovitz, *Franfurter Rabbinen* (Frankfort/Main 1884-85) 3: 65; 4: 23-24. See also Friedberg [n. 26]: 12-15. On Polish rabbis of Altona-Hamburg-Wandsbek, see Duckesz [n. 33]: 53-59, 63-74; of Metz, BJGL 2 (1900): 38-39; EJ 3: 347-48. For immigrant rabbis of Fürth, see JJLG 6 (1908): 199-209. On Ezekiel Landau, see G. Klemperer's biog., Eng. tr. in HJ 13 (1951): 55-76.
104. Friedberg [n. 26]: 15-18; Horovitz [n. 103] 4: 82; L. Müller, "Aus fünf Jahrhunderten: Beiträge zur Geschichte der jüdischen Gemeinden im Riess," *Zeitschrift des Historischen Vereins für Schwaben und Neuburg* 26 (1899): 133-36; HJ 13 (1951): 71-80; Landshuth [n. 19]: 30-32; Horowitz [n. 2]: 68-69; EJ 3: 491-92; JJLG 6 (1908): 203-7; 14 (1921): 22-24; EJ 1: 875-77, 881-82.
105. For occupations of Polish Jewish immigrants in America, see Stern [n. 32], *pass.*; Rosenbloom [n. 32]. On Mordecai M. Cohen's wealth, cf. Reznikoff [n. 98]; came to America before 1800 (Stern [n. 32]: 29).
106. JFF [n. 90]; Roth [n. 10]: 194-95; Picciotto [n. 14]: 334-35.
107. JFF [n. 12]: 170; Meisl [n. 64]: 207, 316; Jacobson [n. 64]; Freudenthal [n. 45].
108. Maimon [n. 4], esp.: 73 ("a Polish Jew residing in Berlin [was] received in the best houses"); Wessely [n. 4]. See also biogs. of Polish *maskilim* in Klausner [n. 3], *pass.*
109. Roth [n. 10]: 191 n. 3, 195; Jolowicz [n. 67]: 183; E. Hintze,

Katalog . . . Ausstellung . . . Schlesien (Breslau 1929): 39; Picciotto [n. 106] (Simon Solomon); PAJHS 21 (1913): 215.
110. Brann [n. 8]: 74 (members had such names as Kalisch, Littauer, Lubliner, and Plessner); *Festschrift* [n. 13]: xx; Roth [n. 10]: 298; MJHSE 6 (1962): 178-83; JFF [n. 12]: 162; Gronemann [n. 21] (H sect.): 45 (Copenhagen); Meisl [n. 64]: 316-18, 343, 396-97, 401-2; Reznikoff [n. 13], *pass.*; PAJHS 50 (1960): 55.
111. To be sure, when too many teachers from Poland arrived in Paderborn and competed with local teachers, strong opposition arose against them. Likewise, J. Emden, unsuccessful candidate for rabbi of Altona-Hamburg-Wandsbek, became an opponent of immigrant rabbi of that community and was generally critical of immigrant rabbis and teachers.
112. On emigration of German and Austrian Jews to America, see M. Wischnitzer, *To Dwell in Safety* (Philadelphia 1948): 3-36. On conversion movement in Prussia, see A. Menes in *Yivo: Historische Schriften* [Y] 1 (Warsaw 1929): 375-404. On Holland, see N. Robinson, ed., *European Jewry Ten Years after the War* (New York 1956): 220; *Festskrift* [n. 21]: 253-57.
113. From branches of only one family of Polish Jews who went to Germany variously c. 1700, such diverse personalities originated as Moses Mendelssohn, Gabriel Riesser, and possibly Karl Marx, another of whose ancestors, Rabbi Moses Aaron Lvov of Trier, was from Lemberg. Freudenthal [n. 19]: 37, 117, 271; M. Wolsteiner, *Genealogische Übersicht über einige Zweige der Nachkommenschaft des Rabbi Meir Katzenellenbogen von Padua* (Berlin 1898): 3; *Festskrift* [n. 21]: 277-89.

Index

Names of localities in Eastern Europe denote emigrants' places of origin. Names of localities in western countries denote immigrants' places of settlement. Since Germany and Poland are mentioned on almost every page, they are not indexed; however, specific regions in Germany (e.g. Western Germany) and Poland (e.g. Lithuania, Volhynia) are listed.

157

Index

159

Index

Moses A. Shulvass is Distinguished Service Professor of Jewish History and chairman of the department of graduate studies at Spertus College of Judaica, Chicago. He is a native of Poland where he received his rabbinical degree in Warsaw (1930). Rabbi Shulvass, who also earned a Ph.D. degree at Friedrich Wilhelms University, Berlin (1934), is the author of six previous books and of numerous articles in Jewish scholarly and literary journals.

Charles H. Elam edited the manuscript. The book was designed by Don Ross. The type face for the text is Linotype Caledonia designed by W. A. Dwiggins about 1937. The display face is Bulmer cut by William Martin about 1790 for William Bulmer.

The text is printed on Bradford Book paper; the book is bound in Interlaken's Arco Linen cloth over binders' boards. Manufactured in the United States of America.